T0149510

It's a Race against Time

Edward Mutema

WESTBOW
PRESS®
A DIVISION OF THOMAS NELSON
& ZONDERVAN

All Bible quotations are from the ESV unless indicated otherwise.

Scripture quotations marked (ESV) are from the ESV® Bible (The Holy Bible, English Standard Version®), copyright © 2001 by Crossway, a publishing ministry of Good News Publishers. Used by permission. All rights reserved.

Scripture quotations marked (GNT) are from the Good News Translation in Today's English Version- Second Edition Copyright © 1992 by American Bible Society. Used by Permission.

Scripture quotations from THE MESSAGE. Copyright © by Eugene H. Peterson 1993, 1994, 1995, 1996, 2000, 2001, 2002. Used by permission of NavPress. All rights reserved. Represented by Tyndale House Publishers, Inc.

Scripture taken from the New King James Version®. Copyright © 1982 by Thomas Nelson. Used by permission. All rights reserved.

Scripture quotations marked (NIV) are taken from the Holy Bible, New International Version®, NIV®. Copyright © 1973, 1978, 1984, 2011 by Biblica, Inc.™ Used by permission of Zondervan. All rights reserved worldwide. www.zondervan.com The "NIV" and "New International Version" are trademarks registered in the United States Patent and Trademark Office by Biblica, Inc.™

WestBow Press books may be ordered through booksellers or by contacting:

WestBow Press
A Division of Thomas Nelson & Zondervan
1663 Liberty Drive
Bloomington, IN 47403
www.westbowpress.com
1 (866) 928-1240

Because of the dynamic nature of the Internet, any web addresses or links contained in this book may have changed since publication and may no longer be valid. The views expressed in this work are solely those of the author and do not necessarily reflect the views of the publisher, and the publisher hereby disclaims any responsibility for them.

Any people depicted in stock imagery provided by Thinkstock are models, and such images are being used for illustrative purposes only. Certain stock imagery © Thinkstock.

ISBN: 978-1-5127-7860-1 (sc)
ISBN: 978-1-5127-7861-8 (hc)
ISBN: 978-1-5127-7859-5 (e)

Library of Congress Control Number: 2017903623

Print information available on the last page.

WestBow Press rev. date: 03/20/2017

This book is dedicated to a dear brother Chris Owens. He kept the faith. He finished his race.

Acknowledgements

A big thank you to the love of my life, Tererai, and our wonderful children, Bongai, Gareth, and Janice (Kuzi). You have been supportive all the way. Great team!

To Dr Phineas Dube who finished his race in 2017 and is now in eternity; and his wife Tebbie- faithful servants of God.

To Jan Owens, a great woman of God.

Contents

Author's Confession...xi

Chapter 1   It's a Race against Time 1

Chapter 2   Set the Agenda...7

Chapter 3   It Is an Obstacle Race 17

Chapter 4   It Is Time to Let Go 23

Chapter 5   Work While It Is Day 28

Chapter 6   Live Life with Intensity...................................34

Chapter 7   Focus on the Finishing Line...........................38

Chapter 8   Time to Pray More 41

Chapter 9   Time to Serve More 46

Chapter 10   Time to Mature More 50

Chapter 11   Time to Love More 55

Chapter 12   It Is Time to Forgive More 62

Chapter 13   Time to Endure More than Ever....................66

Chapter 14   Time to Prioritize More 74

Chapter 15   Time to Not Procrastinate 77

Chapter 16   Time to Give More Than Ever 89

Chapter 17   Time to Be Content and Worry No More.....94

Chapter 18   Time to Invest Wisely.................................. 102

Chapter 19   Be a Winner 116

Chapter 20   Equip Yourself... 126

Chapter 21   Be an Example.. 131

Chapter 22   Work Smart... 134

Chapter 23   The Three-Year Assignment Strategy 145

Chapter 24   Choose Life 151

Chapter 25   Focus on Your Destination 153

Chapter 26   Where will You Spend Eternity?

                    (Your Long-term Investment)..................... 160

The End 169

Author's Confession

Great opportunities to be productive and useful were missed many times during my journey. Some were deliberate, and others were due to purposeless existence that was fanned by a lack of exposure to the great examples from men and women of faith, who lived their life with intensity. My world at one time was so parochial that planning was always in the short term and not in the medium and long term. Personal development remained stunted at times, until the eureka moment came and I awoke from my slumber.

Sadly, this narrative represents many men and women who are content with survival, being there and not being somewhere. But all of us can change. The realisation that we are here for a purpose must drive all of us to doing that which we were called to do with intensity. The reason? We are racing against time, and it will soon be over. I now want today to matter. I seek to accomplish all I can today. I want to plan for it, review it, and never repeat the same mistakes today that brought yesterday. Today becomes a lifetime. Today becomes intense. Today becomes purposeful. Today heralds opportunities to serve God and other fellow human beings.

It means I set the agenda, and I do all I can to complete it. I prioritise, stay focused, and deal with the unfinished business. David was aware of the importance of this day when he was inspired to write, "This is the day that the Lord has made, let us rejoice and be glad in it" (Ps. 118:24). The cumulative effect of having such an attitude on one day is awesome. It is a revolution and changes you for life.

We don't own time, but it is made available to all of us in equal amounts. The moment babies scream out of their mothers' womb, their allocation is already determined, and the number of days they are on this planet are set. As Jesus said to his followers, "It is not for you to know times or seasons that the Father has fixed by his own authority" (Acts 1:7). That is when the race begins. The quality of their lives and the achievements they make will depend on how they handle this precious gift. The environment, their upbringing, and their awareness and personal development from the beginning will determine their joy, happiness, success, and contentment on the road to another time zone: eternity. And when they finally say goodbye to this planet, well-known as death, they will take on a new address: a heaven postcode!

Managing one's lifetime is a serious business. It requires all the technical competencies of the most successful corporate executive. It requires planning, goal setting, and a broad vision of where we are going, how we are going to get there, and the steps needed to achieve our goals.

This enterprise called life is huge. If we fail to use the opportunities that come our way, we will live miserable existences with nothing to show for it at the end of Project Life. This is why it is a race against time. Time will continue to tick away. It won't wait, and it won't come back. What we lost has been lost, but it is in our power to manage it, to slot in every day those things that we want for the success of our enterprise. We can prioritise on the major things in life. We can exclude all that does not enhance a life filled with purpose and meaning. It is in our power, and God has promised to be alongside us should we need help of a supernatural kind.

We have an example of Jesus, whose active working life was three years. In that time, he lived each day with such intensity that he refused to be sidetracked by his detractors. He remained focused and in three years was able to accomplish the task. He left a bunch of trained and competent followers who were able to carry on his legacy forever. When we live life with intensity, it will make a difference to those whom we encounter. We are bound to influence others. The mark of a successful purposeful enterprise is that even when we are no more, the work will carry on and will multiply a million times.

This book suggests strategies that can help us to live today and tomorrow, vigilant and conscious of what we have to do in order to fulfil our lives' purpose within the time that we are given.

Chapter 1

It's a Race against Time

By the time this book is published, I will be a few months away from my sixty-fifth birthday. A few years ago, it hit me that this roller coaster called life was like a juggernaut – unstoppable – but I could do something to capitalize on the rest of my unlived life. I have been grateful to God for the opportunities, for carrying me when the road seemed rough, for bringing onto my path family and friends who have been there for me. But this sense of urgency hit me like a ton of bricks as I realized how Jesus – the greatest teacher, coach, and motivator – did it. He was an example for us all to emulate. He was conscious of his race, and he responded to it by living and behaving like a great competitor. This is why this chapter is so important. It helps us peep into Jesus's mindset, vision, and mission, and how these affected his outlook on how he was to conduct his Father's business. It is the same mindset that we should have. It is a paradigm shift that will impact our response to the race of life. Let's sample some of these nuggets.

We are all aliens. As the Bible puts it, we are sojourners like the people of Israel. In modern terminology, we'd be called travellers. We're on the move, transient and not permanent. The more we drum this in our heads, the more it will affect the way we conduct ourselves today, tomorrow, and always. We need to have this sojourner mindset.

Jesus had three years to teach, preach, do miracles, and complete his mission. And he did it, on the dot. Moses had forty years to do the job at the age of eighty. He was refused entry into the Promised Land, but he guided the nation of Israel to the outskirts of Canaan. Paul had spent years of misguided living as a professor who had refused to profess Christ, but after the Damascus Road experience, he was set on the road to accomplishing God's purposes. He ended up in Rome under house arrest, but not before he impacted at least twenty-five million people in the Greco-Roman world. Wow!

You don't have to act big to impact the world. A boy's lunch, a mere two loaves of bread and two fish, fed thousands with a blessing from Jesus. The boy shared at the appropriate time.

How much time do you have to do what God sent you to accomplish? Are you constantly planning for it? Can you envisage the end from the beginning? Jesus was clear. He cried, "It is finished," heralding the end of his active duty.

When we know how important our mission is, we will place it in the urgent tray for us to deal with it. Reflect on your relationships, especially your marriage. Are there issues to sort out? Are you living worlds apart even though officially you are supposed to be man and wife? Can you sort it out now while you still have your being? Why not enjoy each other as God intended?

Jesus did not mince words when he said, "We must work the works of him who sent me while it is day; night is coming, when no one can work" (John 9:4). We must work with a sense of urgency, like we are going to board the next flight.

Jesus knew this from the start. He had three years to complete his mission. This wasn't much, but he crammed everything in that time, and on one Friday afternoon, while hanging on a wooden cross, it is recorded that when Jesus had received the sour wine, he said, "It is finished!" Then he bowed his head and released his spirit (John 19:30).

It is not so with many of us. Twenty, thirty, forty, or even sixty years down the line, we have nothing to show for all these years but loads of unfinished business – unforgiveness, hate, worry, and stinking baggage that we continue to carry. It's sad, but it is never too late. You can start now. At least plan for the next three years, as Jesus did. Read that book that you have always wanted to read. Embark on that course that you left halfway through. Sort out your relationship with that errant son who has dogged you all along. Forgive the husband who has been a pain in your life. Love the love of your life, who you have treated like trash all these years. Present your body as a living sacrifice before your Maker, and make a commitment to do what he tells you. See what happens. The impact you are

3

going to make is phenomenal. Your life will never be the same again, and many will enjoy the benefits long after you are gone. Jesus did this, along with many heroes of the faith. They turned the world upside down, and lives continue to be transformed.

I guess this means being aware of your purpose, planning for it, and persisting until the job is done. You remain focused, committed, and dedicated to the task. You can only do this for a limited duration of time. For many of us, it ends at seventy years, and for some it's a little bit longer.

> Our days may come to seventy years,
> or eighty, if our strength endures;
> yet the best of them are but trouble and sorrow,
> for they quickly pass, and we fly away.
> If only we knew the power of your anger!
> Your wrath is as great as the fear that is your due.
> Teach us to number our days,
> that we may gain a heart of wisdom. (Ps.
> 0:1–12 NIV)

However long you have, the important thing is to do it within your time. He does not increase the hours of the day; they remain twenty-four for everybody. It is how we use those hours that will determine whether we beat the clock of life.

We have to work today. Day means during our active life when we are still breathing. Night is the end, when the curtain comes down, tolls are silent, and night beckons. It's time to sleep until the morning, when shadows fade away and we land on planet heaven. We can no longer mumble and stumble, but silently the clock stops, and we wake up to another life.

So rise up! This is the time to accomplish your goals, to do that which God intended to accomplish through you. Jesus did, Paul did, and many others did. So go for it and start now. It's a race against time – God's time.

Plan, change, and implement. Jesus came up with a deliberate strategy. He was clear about what he wanted to achieve, how he was going to do it, and his final destination. He knew the end from the beginning, and when you are racing against time, this becomes crucial. What is your plan? For the followers of Jesus, they had to change before they were able to implement the task at hand. They were changed by God's Spirit, God's Word, and their interaction with Jesus. Finally, they did what they were told. Implementation was the key to fulfilling the endgame.

Change guarantees that you are able and willing to adapt to the urgent situations. It can never be business as usual. Each passing day becomes an opportunity to implement the plan. Paul puts it this way: "However, I consider my life worth nothing to me; my only aim is to finish the race and complete the task the Lord Jesus has given me – the task of testifying to the good news of God's grace" (Acts 20:24 NIV).

It is worth reflecting on your task. What is it that you are convinced is your purpose on planet earth? What is your strategy, your plan? Many people spend their lifetimes working out what it is they are here for, and when they don't know where they are going, any road will do. That is a recipe for disaster and a wasted life. Stop now and think. Write on paper all that you think you are meant to do here on earth. Go ahead and tackle each one of those with passion and commitment. You may have a few years to live, but do it anyway; it will bring fulfilment. If it is teaching others, go ahead and do it. If it is encouraging others, avail yourself.

CHAPTER 2

Set the Agenda

Just like any athlete, we must know what race we are in and what is required for us to compete effectively. Our to-do lists should be obvious from the beginning before we embark on the training and eventual running or competing in the race. We cannot expect others outside the race to determine what we are going to do, and we are all in this race of life. We are all expected to be clear as to what we are going to do to successfully complete the race. It is our agenda, and we must be responsible for it. In this race, one of the greatest life coaches that ever lived has clearly presented guidelines we must follow if we are to run competitively. But we must embrace the guidelines, the advice, the warnings, and the encouragements.

There are certain skills required in order for us to become competent. There are certain disciplines, attitudes, and personalities that must be part of the agenda that you can ignore at your peril. All this is for the taking and is clearly spelled out in the manual.

You are in charge, and God from the beginning has given us that responsibility. David says, "Yet you have made him a little lower than the heavenly beings and crowned him with glory and honour. You have given him dominion over the works of your hands; you have put all things under his feet" (Ps. 8:5–6). We are unique. We are royal and at the pinnacle of God's leadership circle. Whatever we decide to do with our time, resources, and talents within the allocated time frame of our lives, we can determine the course of events. Be it our personal agenda, family agenda, or relational agenda, we have the power to set it. We have the capacity to drive the momentum and seek the achievement of our goals when the clock of our lives stops ticking. No blame game – we are accountable, responsible.

How do you determine what is important? How do you decipher which voices to listen to, which friends to associate with? How do you discriminate between the good, the bad, and the ugly on your agenda? You decide. You are the master of it. You have been given the power to do it. Many of us have messed it up because we have failed to take responsibility. We have refused to be accountable.

The men of Isaachar in the Bible were known for one thing: "From Issachar, men who understood the times and knew what Israel should do – 200 chiefs, with all their relatives under their command" (1 Chron. 12:32 NIV). This is an important skill: knowing what to do and when to do it. Many people have been caught up doing the wrong thing at the right time, or the right thing at the wrong time. It demands wisdom to do what these men of Isaachar did. They had garnered so much experience that it became something for which they were known.

Such understanding meant that they were able to respond to the situation accordingly. Their agenda reflected the greatest priorities that would enable them to achieve their objectives. They always knew what time it was and the appropriate way to act. You can only understand when you have knowledge about a certain subject. This is our greatest challenge. Whatever we include on our agenda, we must contribute to the realisation of our goals and objectives within the time frame that we have. Whatever we do must be informed by the knowledge that God spoke to Hosea about: "My people are destroyed for lack of knowledge" (Hos. 4:6 NJKV).

A man called Jabez prayed a significant prayer. This was part of his agenda presented to God. "Jabez cried out to the God of Israel, 'Oh, that you would bless me and enlarge my territory! Let your hand be with me, and keep me from harm so that I will be free from pain'" (1 Chron. 4:10 NIV). And God granted his request.

He was not content with what he had. He saw beyond the horizon, realised that he had great potential, and was keen to realise that potential within his lifetime. God wants to see our agenda in black and white: what it is that we want as we travel this road, as we race against time. We need to spell it out. "Do not be anxious about anything, but in every situation, by prayer and petition, with thanksgiving, present your requests to God (Phil. 4:6 NIV). The "things to do" idea started with God. He has always been keen to give an ear to his people when they go through trying times during the race of life. He has always been at the ready to intervene when the going seems to get tough. In fact, when the going gets tough, God expects us to cast our cares to him because he is a caring God and is ready to help.

Set your broad agenda on personal relationships, on behaviour, on integrity. Be the person God wants you to be and become. And Paul presents guidelines on behaviour for people who are racing against time:

> Don't waste your time on useless work, mere busywork, the barren pursuits of darkness. Expose these things for the sham they are. It's a scandal when people waste their lives on things they must do in the darkness where no one will see. Rip the cover off those frauds and see how attractive they look in the light of Christ.
> Wake up from your sleep,
> Climb out of your coffins;
> Christ will show you the light!
> So watch your step. Use your head. Make the most of every chance you get. These are desperate times!

Don't live carelessly, unthinkingly. Make sure you understand what the Master wants. (Eph. 5:11–17 MSG)

It's your show, and you are in charge. You will be surprised how many people let go and allow others to dictate the way they should go. If you are not clear on purpose, direction, and passion, then anything goes. Before you know it, you are lying on your death bed, regretful and sad. Say no. Today, the world is your oyster. You can access the world from your mobile;

resource yourself from the comfort of your home. Go on – start now and determine your destiny.

Growing up in my village was a big deal for me. It was the most glorious experience one could have. Contentment was the key word. But my mother had an agenda: she wanted me to do well, to excel in life. At age ten, I made contact with a pen pal from South Africa who was doing a degree at the University of Cape Town. When he visited us in the village with a group of other students, I was elated. It was a dream come true. He was white, and I was a young black boy. My mum cooked for them, and to crown it all, he said, "Edward, you never know. One day you may visit South Africa."

Long after they had gone, my mother prophetically said, "Who knows. If you do well and do what Jesus says, you may end up in England!" Wow! It was unbelievable then, but my mother had set the agenda for her son.

Years later, not only did I visit South Africa, but I was in Cape Town for meetings as the CEO of the Bible Society of Zimbabwe. England was where I studied, ending up at the prestigious London School of Economics and Political Science. The boy from the village, with his agenda set, was able to realise his dreams. This was long before I learnt about setting goals. Sometimes I think I simply did it without putting a title to it!

You see, from the cradle to the grave, you are in charge of your life. You determine what is and what is not to happen.

You are the driver; God expects you to be one. You assess the situation and come up with what needs to be done in order for you to realise your dreams, in order for you to do what you were destined to do during the time allocated to you by the Creator. You either mess up or make up, focus or drift aimlessly like a rolling stone that gathers no moss. But you are smarter than that. You are special. You have unique talents or gifts, and that is the stuff that you need to get things going.

I remember vividly as a teenager when my father pleaded with me. "Edward, can we find time to talk at least once a week, so that I can let you into my life and tell you about myself?" This was a surprise. My father was a disciplinarian; he did not tolerate nonsense from his children. Here he was, inviting me to a focus group discussion. The few meetings we had were the most revealing and made me appreciate who he was and his agenda for me. At one of the meetings, he prophetically said, "Edward, one day you will be like Joseph in the Bible. You will look after your brothers and sisters, if you do what Jesus tells you." You see, as the last born, his words became true. It was a joy to be a member of the family who was able to facilitate the development of some of my relatives. And my brothers and sisters did end up staying in our house at one time or another. First, my father had to set an agenda for his son, which was to be realised before and after he had gone to be with Jesus. Goal achieved!

Set the agenda now. Jesus set his, and within three years, he ticked all the boxes and said goodbye to his band of followers. They were left mesmerised, and even when they were told that he had risen, they could not believe it.

It has never been on God's agenda to ambush us, to suddenly come up with something that he has not clearly warned us about. In his great manual of life, it is spelt out. He expects us to take heed, put it on our agenda, and strive to do as we are told. Many people have deliberately ignored this, to their peril. Broken marriages, unfulfilling lives, unforgiveness, stunted growth, and nations have fallen because of lack of righteousness. "Righteousness exalts a nation, but sin condemns any people" (Prov. 14:34 NIV).

Time and Tide Wait for No Man

On our thirtieth anniversary, we checked into a hotel just by the beach. Each morning, we would observe the powdery, sandy beach. This did not last long because as we watched, slowly the waters crept in towards the shore. Slowly but persistently, the sands were overwhelmed. Soon even the boulders by the sea shore were engulfed. The tide was in. This happened at the same time every day, without fail, no excuses. It didn't matter who was on that shoreline; sooner or later, people would be drowned by the tide, as it did what it timeously had to do. In winter, spring, and summer, the pattern is the same. You cannot fight against this phenomenon; it is fixed and will happen whether we like it or not.

This is a simple concept which was at the heart of what Jesus taught. It's a realisation that there are things we cannot change. All we need to do is to be ready to respond when they do occur. If we sat on that beach and ignored the tide, soon we would be history. The same is true with time. Our allocation of it comes and goes. If we are unable to do that which we are meant to do within the allocation we have, tough. For some of us, it is a mere few years; for others, it's twenty, forty, fifty, or even one hundred forty (in the case of the Indonesian man). However long or short, time will soon pass away. Either we decided to ignore it at our own peril, or we take heed and live fulfilling lives in accordance with what we were meant to be and to become. It is our choice, and Jesus and many who have gone before us laboured this point. Writing this chapter is part of my desire to do that which God wants me to do. If these pages can influence a life for the better, I will be pleased because I will have done my part.

The good thing with the tide is that we are made aware of the set times when it comes in and goes out. We are given ample time to prepare. Where I live now, there are beach races. I will see cars parked on the beach. Yes, it is possible to do this while the tide is out. When it is time for it to come in, there is no sign of activity on the beach. God has been generous enough to give us warning signs: intermittent alerts on when we can expect the tide to come in, and how we can take precautions. Peter writes that God has decided to delay his tide to allow people to heed the warning signs.

Don't overlook the obvious here, friends. With God, one day is as good as a thousand years, a thousand years as a day. God isn't late with his promise as some measure lateness. He is restraining himself on account of you, holding back the End because he doesn't want anyone lost. He's giving everyone space and time to change. (2 Pet. 2:3 MSG)

We have time to prepare; we can be ready in time. The story of Noah in the Bible is a clear example of people who, for one hundred twenty years, ignored the warnings of Noah. Up to the last minute, even as they drowned, it never sank in that what God had said would come to pass. You bet that there were rich, poor, the educated, the learned, and many others. All of them failed to heed a simple instruction. Don't we all at times?

No wonder Jesus's schedule was packed. Every day he wanted to do that which he had come to do, while there was still time. Very soon he would no longer be able to do so. How conscious are you of the impending tide of our lives? This book is a rallying call to us to reflect on our response to this life, to this time that he has generously given us.

The Tide

In the distant horizon yonder,
As the sun drowns in the golden sky beneath,
See the ripples rushing towards the sandy show,
Struggling to make headway.
The sand fights back;

CHAPTER 3

It Is an Obstacle Race

"I press on toward the goal" Philippians 3:14

From the word go, our race is littered with obstacles. Consider a typical day in the life of Jesus. He slept late after preaching, healing, and comforting people. Early in the morning before dawn, he was on his knees praying. Soon after, crowds were milling around him, waiting to hear him preach. As he started his day, his opponents were strategically placed amongst the crowd, in the synagogue, in the temple, and at important occasions, simply to ascertain what he was up to. They analysed, criticised, and jeered every move. Even when he was home in his house, helping the crowds that had come in, they watched from a distance. Every step of the way, on a given day, Jesus encountered every obstacle imaginable.

But he knew he was in a race. He knew there was limited time, and he focused on the goal rather than the distractions that popped up unexpectedly. He had three years to accomplish his mission. Instead of dwelling on the unimportant, he saw the bigger picture beyond the critics, naysayers, and distractors. He

Edward Mutema

did what he had been called to do. So must we. When people dismiss us every which way, when we are faced with mountains of criticisms along the way, when our very close friends and relations refuse to see it, we plod on and persist until we finish the race. It's tough but worthwhile. We are men and women on a mission. We have no time to waste, day in and day out.

Here is an example of how Jesus overcame one obstacle in one given day.

> And a man was there with a withered hand. And they asked him, "Is it lawful to heal on the Sabbath?"-so that they might accuse him. (Matt. 12:10)

When Jesus healed the man, the religious leaders were furious and began planning how they were going to get rid of him.

A few observations here. When Jesus got into the meeting place, there were already critics waiting to throw a salvo at him. Second, Jesus kept to the narrative of need. Anything to save life was paramount. His response was already in place, and he anticipated what was going to happen. Third, he shrugged off the naysayers, and he went on to do good and heal the person. Fourth, the plotters began to seriously consider stopping Jesus in his tracks. Fifth, the man was freed from his illness, and thus mission accomplished.

Jesus could have stopped to argue, refused to do the right thing, or gone away sad and discouraged. He could have lost the plot, but he didn't. He kept focused on his mission. He

18

knew there was no time to dally. So must we, daily. Does this remind you of someone, something, and some place where this happened? Always anticipate this. Prepare for it and gather courage and do the right thing. Our race is littered with obstacles. We may not see where we are going, but what matters is knowing where we are going and doing all we can to get there in the time allocated to us.

In another incident, Jesus had come home. He found the home packed with all sorts of people from the door. There was no room, and he started preaching. As he did so, the roof was broken, and a lame man was lowered through the roof. Jesus healed the person in the presence of his critics, who accused him of going against God's laws. Jesus healed the person anyway. He was not distracted and overcame the obstacle. Wow!

As we go through life, this becomes the pattern of our lives as we race against time. It seems that the obstacles intensify as if to obstruct us from the vision of seeing tomorrow and the scarcity of time. This requires a dogged determination to carry on despite the setbacks, to resolve to complete our God-given mission. Many before us have done it, and we are no exceptions. What an encouragement!

Although we will encounter hurdles along the way, we need to stick it out. This means enduring the gruelling moments, the lonely times, and the enduring hardships. We shouldn't be weary, and we should take the bull by its horns because we cannot give up now. Jesus did not. He persevered and endured until the end.

This is how the Message Bible puts it.

> Do you see what this means – all these pioneers who
> blazed the way, all these veterans cheering us on? It
> means we'd better get on with it. Strip down, start
> running – and never quit! No extra spiritual fat, no
> parasitic sins. Keep your eyes on *Jesus*, who both began
> and finished this race we're in. Study how he did it.
> Because he never lost sight of where he was headed –
> that exhilarating finish in and with God – he could
> put up with anything along the way: Cross, shame,
> whatever. And now he's *there*, in the place of honor,
> right alongside God. When you find yourselves flagging
> in your faith, go over that story again, item by item, that
> long litany of hostility he plowed through. *That* will
> shoot adrenaline into your souls! (Heb. 12:1–3 MSG)

The great hero of the faith, Paul of Tarsus, shares his
experiences like this.

> "In every way we're troubled but not crushed, frustrated
> but not in despair, persecuted but not abandoned, struck
> down but not destroyed. We are always carrying around
> the death of Jesus in our bodies, so that the life of Jesus
> may be clearly shown in our bodies. While we are alive,
> we are constantly being handed over to death for Jesus'
> sake, so that the life of Jesus may be clearly shown in
> our mortal bodies. And so death is at work in us, but
> life is at work in you. (2 Cor. 4:8–12 NIV)

For Paul, this was the new normal in his race: always outside his comfort zone. What does your race look like? Don't be fooled; it has never been easy. The key is to look beyond the struggle, to realise that obstacles are part of the process that will see us through. They will mould us, shape us, and make us into what God intended for us. No pain, no gain.

Consider the story of Joseph. He was a dreamer in his infancy, abandoned in a pit by his brothers. He was sold as a slave to the Egyptians and ended up in prison for suspected rape in Pharaoh's house. In thirteen years, Joseph had experienced the hurts and pains that some adults experience in a full lifetime. But he persisted, and he is reckoned to be the man who made it possible for the nation of Israel to remain intact. And 430 years later, the nation of Israel left for the Promised Land in accordance with what God had promised. Obstacles are for a purpose, but they will always come. It's unsettling, and you cannot change them; it is a fact of life. But the greatest benefit is what they bring, how they fashion and mould one's character, and how they can change the course of history. Today we prefer to call them challenges. Many heroes of the faith faced them head-on as if to say, "Bring them on," each time they sensed challenges raising their ugly heads.

I have gone through life-threatening challenges. They were not pleasant, but they have made me who I am now. They raised my spiritual temperature to a level where each day, I am aware that it could be the end. I am aware that the finishing line in my race can suddenly appear from nowhere. The clock can stop at any time. What matters is my readiness, my ability

CHAPTER 4

It Is Time to Let Go

A lifetime is impossible.
A day is all you have
To love, to hold, and to cherish.
Spoil them when you can.
Depart you will;
Who knows when,
Who knows how.
Plan to go.
Let your life be one goodbye.
Adios!

We should never be taken by surprise. Always be ready and get prepared. Jesus was a master at this and taught his followers, "Watch therefore, for you know neither the day nor the hour" (Matt. 25:3 ESV). It's spot-on. No one knows. Scientists have predicted earthquakes, floods, hurricanes, and other natural calamities for ages, but they are never precise. What matters is for us to be ready. It's an open secret that a big earthquake will hit California one day. All that people in downtown Los Angeles can do is to be ready.

We are all racing against time, and we don't know when the big clock of life will stop. But we can make arrangements calmly and deliberately. Rebuild relationships where they are struggling because of our unforgiveness, hate, and jealousy. Restore a broken marriage tittering on the verge of collapse. Sort out a moral relapse issue that has eroded our integrity, or regain friends and family who seem to have drifted so far. We can plan to enjoy quality time with those whom we have not seen for ages, and above all, we can become new from inside.

This process of being ready all the time is the key to embracing the difficult times when they arise, be it through a terminal illness, an unforeseen horrific accident that leaves us limbless, or a tragedy too ghastly to contemplate. At the back of our minds, we should know that this life is transient. We should always have what I said earlier, a sojourner mentality. We are travellers en route to somewhere. When the big *it* happens, we are ready.

When my mother decided to leave me after hours of surgery, I had the opportunity to talk to her a day before she said goodbye. Here was a woman of God who had prepared me for life from when I was a little boy. She had always pointed me to the truth who is Jesus Christ. When I made a decision to follow him, half her battle had been won. On her death bed, I had the guts to say to her, "You can go now, Mama. You have accomplished what you prayed for. I am here, and I know Christ." This was not the easiest of encounters. But it's true she had prepared me for life. She too was prepared to go now. It took me a month to realise the gaping hole in my life. As my friend who recently lost his mum said to me, part of me died with her.

It's no wonder why Jesus classifies those who are not ready as foolish, and those who are ready as wise. Reading this chapter is a reminder to you that you ought to be ready. In fact, we are told God has decided to delay the end in order to allow those who are not ready to do so This is worth repeating:

> Don't overlook the obvious here, friends. With God, one day is as good as a thousand years, a thousand years as a day. God isn't late with his promise as some measure lateness. He is restraining himself on account of you, holding back the End because he doesn't want anyone lost. He's giving everyone space and time to change. (2 Pet. 3:9 MSG)

The name of the game of life is preparation, preparation, preparation. Sometimes I still struggle to prepare. The tendency is to put it off for another day; procrastination creeps in through the back door. But we have to fight this. We have to have the sense of urgency. Life is here today and gone tomorrow. We must see the end from the beginning. The heroes of the faith in the Bible did so. Abraham saw the promised Jerusalem before he got there. Why not arrange for your funeral service and make up the guest list? Why not write your funeral speech?

Thank God for your brother-in-law or sister-in-law before they show up. Why not celebrate in faith your impending birthdays before they arrive? Why not enjoy the joys of heaven today in anticipation of the impending banquet in heaven?

Each day is preparation day. Our walk, talk, and behaviour must be geared towards readiness. The good thing is that we cannot run away from the end, however, rich, poor, intelligent, or foolish. The destination is the same, and the preparation time is allocated fairly. So why wait? Do it now, today. Be ready. You cannot stop the clock, but when the clock of your life stops, it will be no surprise.

Why not resolve issues if you can? Why not forgive that child who hurt you deeply? Why not seek God's forgiveness for the moral sin that has caused you hurt in past? Why not do now that which you have been postponing for years? The race will become easier and more fun.

One key thing is to realise that all these friends and relations will not be with us any longer when the race is up. You'd better practice now to allow them to live on their own. It is like when athletes go into the athletes' village: no more family – they are on their own. This is what you must prepare for. We all must. You must get used to seeing them do things in their own way, to watching them blunder. Pick them up when they stumble, and groom them for a life without you. Yes, without you. You will soon be no more. You will be watching from the grandstands. You will spur them on; that is when you are no more. So let go. Do it gently, peacefully, and lovingly.

They remain dear to you for now. Soon they will love God's embrace. You will only be a memory far away, a flicker of light soon past. A wife loved but left, a husband dear but distant. So let go now. Time beckons, and the end is nigh. The trumpet sounds; the call is heard. You will soon pass, with a life lived in joy. Lovers are truly loving.

But Jesus has his say. He too had his mother, sisters, and brothers. On a dark Friday night, he called, "It is finished," and he gave up the ghost. He died and left for a better world. You too are on your way, so let go. You will be on your own when the time comes. The flicker will drown for the last time, and you will fly away to a home where joy shall never end. What should you do on this last mile? Have pen and paper ready, your mind and thoughts alert. Think on these things.

CHAPTER 5

Work While It Is Day

As long as it is day, we must do the works of him who
sent me. Night is coming, when no one can work.

—John 9:4 (NIV)

The work Jesus did was intentional. He did not depart from the
original script that his father gave him. The narrative remained
the same until the end. As we do business daily, it is important
to know what we are here on earth to do. What is it that is
crucial as we race against time?

This was what mattered most to Jesus. It defined his mission
on earth. It enabled him to accomplish what he was sent here
to do. He valued work and was a doer. He was not contented
to live in the comfort zone. Once his passion was birthed, he
went for it daily. He was stamina filled, purpose driven, and
time conscious. He believed in doing it now. The important
became the urgent as he raced against the time that God had
allocated to him.

The reason Jesus gave was because the night is coming.
The night represented closure, a time when what we want

to do could not be done because the end had come. Such realisation meant that he could prioritise and concentrate on those things worth doing for the time available. Procrastination was impossible because there was no tomorrow. Today was the day to accomplish tomorrow, if you were not to be caught napping when the time comes.

The Bible is very dramatic about the end. Jesus says, "But concerning that day and hour no one knows, not even the angels of heaven, nor the Son, but the Father only" (Matt. 24:36,). It comes upon us all of a sudden, when we are least prepared. Jesus puts it into its historical perspective: "Just as it was in the days of Noah, so will it be in the days of the Son of Man. They were eating and drinking and marrying and being given in marriage, until the day when Noah entered the ark, and the flood came and destroyed them all" (Luke 17:26–27 ESV).

It will be business as usual, and then suddenly it's nightfall, and nothing can no longer be done. The day will not come back. The end will be as planned, period. It's scary in a way but hopeful, because the warning signs are everywhere. For Jesus, this was a big deal. This was a matter that prompted him to do more in the time that he had – three years at the most – and he did it. He challenged those of his team who were to remain behind to follow his example. Were they up to the task? Are you?

Are you urgency oriented like Jesus? Are you working on your passion to the maximum for the time you have been allocated? Surely there will be distractions. There will be the urge to do something other than what you do best. May be you have already lost time. But it is now that is important. The next five years should not be the same as the last five years. You are required to work while it is still day. Now – not yesterday, not tomorrow.

How did Jesus use his time? What work did he do? In the chapter on the three-year assignment, we touched on the major activities of Jesus. He prayed. This was high on his agenda. Through prayer he was able to communicate with his father on issues concerning the vital business he had come for. He consulted his father when he wanted to make long-term decisions like choosing his disciples. He asked for assistance when he was faced with a difficult situation, such as when he was called upon to feed the five thousand people who were hungry. He thanked God for his goodness and for the miracle he was going to perform. When he was in the Garden of Gethsemane, facing impending death, he pleaded with his father to intervene. He taught his team and the many crowds that thronged him. He was tireless. From morning until evening, his diary was full of speaking engagements. They ranged from mountaintop sermons, river sermons, teaching by the beach, teaching from the boat, and sometimes teaching casually when he was walking with his disciples. He always taught substance. He used modern methods of storytelling and parables. His audiences were captivated all the time, and he always attracted large crowds who wanted to hang around with him.

He healed people and made them whole. Many came to his surgery, to be restored back to health. This kept him so busy that sometimes he had to withdraw from the crowds in order to pray. This must have been very exhausting. Remember that he had only twelve in his team to begin with. When Jesus talked about working while it was still day, he knew what he was talking about because he had experienced it. Some of his healing episodes were no walkovers. He confronted some of the most dangerous people, like the man from the tombs who could break any chain tied round him. When he confronted Jesus, he hit a brick wall. His powers were neutralised. "Then people went out to see what had happened, and they came to Jesus and found the man from whom the demons had gone, sitting at the feet of Jesus, clothed and in his right mind, and they were afraid" (Luke 8:35–36). This must have been a shattering experience to those who witnessed it. In fact, Jesus was asked to withdraw from the neighbourhood.

Jesus urged his followers to work. His work was specific, focused, and purpose driven. He was to do the work that he had been sent to do, not any other work. We referred to this as our passion, our assignment, what God has called us to do. This is penchant zeal. Work that consumes us must be done under the direction of the one who sent us. Remember Jesus's mission statement: "For the Son of Man came to seek and to save the lost" (Luke 19:10 NIV). Jesus was selfless and did not expect kudos from those for whom he had come to do business. What a great leadership example. Jesus in turn sends his team with this assignment.

Go therefore and make disciples of all nations, baptising

them in the name of the Father, and of the Son and of
the Holy Spirit, teaching them to observe all that I have
commanded you. And behold I am with you always, to
the end of the age. (Matt. 28:19–20)

Making disciples, baptising, and teaching were the key
components of the assignment given to Team Jesus. They are
given to you too, if you believe. No doubt if you don't believe
and are reading this book, you still have a passion. You still want
to excel in order to do the best you can to make a difference
within the time that you have.

Our work has been clarified, and this is the work we need
to pursue every day, just as Jesus worked to do that which his
father sent him to do. Many times we have regarded work as
working for someone, not as working on ourselves. We must
develop ourselves while we have the opportunity. As we do so,
this will affect what we do for others. Jesus was always keen to
emphasise the importance of developing the inner person who
will in turn impact the outside. David says, "I have hidden your
word in my heart that I might not sin against you" (Ps. 119:11
NIV). The word impacts the external environment; what
happens inside affects the quality of the work produced. You
add value to yourself when you work on yourself – this is called
personal development. How much time do you spend working
on yourself during this race against time? What matters is what
kind of a person you will be in the end. Peter sums this up well
by talking about the trials we face on our journey.

These have come so that the proven genuineness of

your faith – of greater worth than gold, which perishes even though refined by fire – may result in praise, glory and honor when Jesus Christ is revealed. (1 Pet. 1:7 NIV)

CHAPTER 6

Live Life with Intensity

Intensity Is Not a State of Mind;
It Is a State of Emotion

Knowing what you are here for, how long you have to accomplish it, and what you ought to do – this is purposeful living. It means shrugging off distractions, however tempting, in order to focus on the race. Today, there is no shortage of things that can steer us off course, be they friends, struggles, botched relationships, and competing forces from the social media.

Jesus was a master at shrugging off distractions. When there was a drive to prop him up as a king, he went underground for the sake of what he had come to do. Populism was not a distraction he entertained. Here is a classic example.

> Very early in the morning, while it was still dark,
> Jesus got up, left the house and went off to a solitary
> place, where he prayed. Simon and his companions

went to look for him, and when they found him, they exclaimed: "Everyone is looking for you!" Jesus replied, "Let us go somewhere else – to the nearby villages – so I can preach there also. That is why I have come." So he traveled throughout Galilee, preaching in their synagogues and driving out demons. (Mark 1:35–36 NIV)

Jesus was like a celebrity. People were looking for him – some to hear him, and others seeking solace in him and wanting to be healed. Simon told Jesus that everyone was looking for him. Jesus could easily have succumbed to this sort of popularity. He didn't. Instead, he refocused his attention on why he was doing what he was doing. He told his followers to accompany him elsewhere so he could teach and preach. This was why he had come, not to be paraded before an audience with an insatiable appetite for glamour and razzmatazz. Wow! That requires focus, clarity, and purpose. His followers had forgotten what made Jesus tick: prayer and sticking to his purpose. They were looking for him at a time when he wanted to resource himself with the power that comes from God. Unfortunately, they did not get it. When you are living a life of purpose, some people will not understand why you do what you do, why you go to the places you go, and why you cannot respond to the glare of publicity that can make you into celebrity. No wonder Jesus was able to accomplish his mission in only three years. You can too. It is when we use every opportunity to do that which we have been called to that we make headway in our mission.

How about this: "Jesus knew that they were about to come and seize him in order to make him king by force; so he went off again to the hills by himself" (John 6:15). Jesus did not give in. He knew his time had not yet come, and the lure to become a king would prematurely scuttle his purpose. When you live on purpose, every activity should, as far as possible, contribute towards the achievement of the mission. This is what Paul struggled to convey to the church in Philippi: he counted all else as dung for the sake of accomplishing that which God had asked him to do. This is a great challenge for us today. In the church, at work, at home, or wherever we are, living with intensity means living on course, on target. It is going for the bull's-eye! That remains your focus, always. Sometimes we stumble, sleep, or slumber. Sometimes we lose track and miss the target. But we rise up, forgetting what lies behind; we strive for the goal. As I am writing, there are issues that have started clogging and blurring my vision. The temptation is to throw in the towel, to protect my integrity and move on as if nothing has happened. But it is important not to allow anything to distract me, to resolve like many before us did and believe it is possible. Yes, we can! Yes, we can meaningfully achieve that which God intended us to accomplish. It is within our grasp. Nothing can deter us if we hold on to the plough and do not look back.

Every opportunity at our disposal becomes critical. Jesus reminds us of someone who used his encounter with people to the max, be it a chance meeting with a revenue official and having dinner with him together with his workmates.

When he was criticised for mingling with sinners, he made a fundamental statement about salvation. On hearing this, Jesus said to them, "It is not the healthy who need a doctor, but the sick. I have not come to call the righteous, but sinners" (Mark 2:17 NIV). By implication, Jesus was saying that God is ready to change those who are trapped in sin – hence his willingness to associate with those who were deemed outcasts. His meeting in the pub was intentional, done for a reason. How many times have we been deliberate in our encounter with people? Is there a purpose?

On another occasion, Jesus invites himself to a revenue officer's house. What happens at the dinner table is astounding. Unprompted, the officer confesses that he had defrauded some people and was willing to repay them four times as much. Jesus pronounced his verdict and said to him, "Today salvation has come to this house, since he is also a son of Abraham" (Luke 19:9). The officer received transformation as a result. This is living life with intensity. This is the challenge that we have on a daily basis from the moment we wake up to the time we sleep and slumber. It is always worth reflecting on how we have made a difference during each mile of the race that is ours. This should be part of our DNA. There should never be a moment when we let life pass by without thinking of using every opportunity to make a difference to ourselves or to those whom we meet and converse with. What a difference this would make if all of us were such inclined and doing just as Jesus did in the three years of his active ministry. No wonder that he was on target. Are you?

CHAPTER 7

Focus on the Finishing Line

"No one who puts his hand to the plow and looks back is fit for the kingdom of God." (Luke 9:62)

You must see the finishing line in order for you to focus on it. It will give you added impetus. Paul sums this up like this.

But whatever were gains to me I now consider loss for the sake of Christ. What is more, I consider everything a loss because of the surpassing worth of knowing Christ Jesus my Lord, for whose sake I have lost all things. I consider them garbage, that I may gain Christ and be found in him, not having a righteousness of my own that comes from the law, but that which is through faith in Christ – the righteousness that comes from God on the basis of faith. I want to know Christ – yes, to know the power of his resurrection and participation in his sufferings, becoming like him in his death, and so, somehow, attaining to the resurrection from the dead.

Not that I have already obtained all this, or have

already arrived at my goal, but I press on to take hold of that for which Christ Jesus took hold of me. Brothers and sisters, I do not consider myself yet to have taken hold of it. But one thing I do: Forgetting what is behind and straining toward what is ahead, I press on toward the goal to win the prize for which God has called me heavenward in Christ Jesus. (Phil. 4:7–15 NIV)

Paul intimated on what every athlete does: they don't look back. They look towards the goal. They become obsessed with winning. Whatever is behind them is not significant anymore. They hardly look at the clock to see how fast they are running. The prize is on the goal, and that is what they concentrate on. Hebrews 12:1–2 says, "Looking to Jesus the founder and perfecter of our faith, who for the joy that was set before him endured the cross, despising the shame, and is seated at the right hand of the throne of God" .

Every race is about winning, and every race is about finishing. Years ago, one Kenyan marathon runner had to crawl towards the finishing line because he was exhausted. He crawled to the finishing line!

When you focus on the finishing line, you do only those things that will enable you to get there. So you must be very selective and only choose to do the things that are significant and that contribute towards your goal. Take marriage, for example. If you are selfish and only want your way, that will not help your relationship. Better to work on your character to allow you to be accommodating to your husband or your wife.

A young man who goes around sleeping with girls will surely find it hard to have a stable relationship. But if he develops his character and lives in accordance with God's word, God will honour him and provide him with someone who will be his partner for life.

CHAPTER 8

Time to Pray More

Watch and pray that you may not enter into temptation.
The spirit indeed is willing, but the flesh is weak.

—Matthew 26:41

Communication has never been so easy in our world today. We have the Internet, mobile phones, Skype, Facebook, Twitter, Instagram. In fact, we cannot resist the urge to communicate every day. On average, some people spend as much as three hours or more a day on social media.

Prayer is communication; it is God talk with the creator of the universe. God is the designer of this magnificent planet and all the other galaxies discovered and yet to be discovered. In a race against time, this must be the deal for everyone in a race to accomplish the mission, a deal for all those living in hope and expectation. We should do more of it, not less. Like Twitter and Facebook, it should come naturally to us. We cannot fear an overdose of it. It should keep us in tune with the one who made us and the one who gave us our assignment. If people can spend twenty-three hours on social media, how much time is spent on God talk? No wonder that Jesus, while praying in Gethsemane before being taken away as a prisoner, was concerned that they could not wait in prayer for just an hour. Many of us are keen communicators on social media and yet spend too little time with the one to whom we owe this life that we have. Reflect on this. How much time do you set aside to commune with God? He is your head coach. He is the one who gives instruction during this race to eternity. Are you in tune with him or not?

Prayer was at the heart of Jesus's life. It was in his DNA. He understood the importance of communication in season and out of season. It was the oil that lubricated his ministry. For him, it was the hotline that made communication between himself and his father easy. He had access through prayer. He was systematic about prayer. He allocated quality time for this activity: early dawn, in the afternoon, in the evening, all night, and when there was immediate need. It was his priority. He even taught the band of twelve how to pray. It was sacrosanct. When he was about to be handed over to his enemies, he went into a garden to pray. He prayed for his disciples before he selected them and just before he departed. At the cross, hanging between two robbers, he prayed, "Forgive them for they know not what they are doing." And Jesus gave a reason why people ought to pray. This was so that they could not enter into temptation. You see, the assignment that we are on has many obstacles. The only way to overcome some of these is the ability to communicate with the God who has all the power and who can turn things around. Prayer does just that. It releases God's power to enable it to deal with whatever challenges we face on a daily basis. Remember that when Peter was in prison, a day before he was to be executed, "the church was praying", and an angel went into prison and released Peter.

There is some supernatural thing that happens when we call upon God to intervene in our affairs. In Jeremiah, God says, "Call to me and I will answer you, and will tell you great and hidden things that you have not known" (Jer. 33:3) We must be persistent in prayer if we are going to ward off the many distractions in our lives. We must have regular closed-door conversations with the creator of the universe.

Communication relieves stress; it is an antidote against stress. This is as good as it gets. Worry can kill you, but when properly managed and directed, worry can lead to your peace, if only you follow the vital steps. Spit it all out. Tell it and don't hide it. Don't bottle up your concerns and worries.

Here is how the Message Bible puts it.

Don't fret or worry. Instead of worrying, pray. Let petitions and praises shape your worries into prayers, letting God know your concerns. Before you know it, a sense of God's wholeness, everything coming together for good, will come and settle you down. It's wonderful what happens when Christ displaces worry at the center of your life" (Phil. 4:6–7)

Peter takes up the same theme: "Cast all your anxiety on him for he cares for you" (1 Pet. 5:7, NIV). This means you literally throw your burdens to him. You must articulate them first and then decide to shove them to the creator. The reason is that we are living in difficult times. The devil is waiting to pounce on those who are the weakest link – those who, because of worries, have become vulnerable.

> Keep a cool head. Stay alert. The Devil is poised to pounce, and would like nothing better than to catch you napping. Keep your guard up. You're not the only ones plunged into these hard times. It's the same with Christians all over the world. So keep a firm grip on the faith. The suffering won't last forever. It won't be long before this generous God who has great plans for us in Christ – eternal and glorious plans they are! – will have you put together and on your feet for good. He gets the last word; yes, he does. (1 Pet. 5:8–11 MSG)

Prayer is a sign of vigilance, alertness, and preparedness. It is the cry to keep connected with the source. It ignites our relationship with our creator and maker. It is communication par excellence. A claim to a vibrant relationship devoid of regular communication is null and void. It is a misnomer, and Jesus proved it. He was the son of God, but he woke up early and went to bed late, praying and in touch with his father. He spent so much time in tune with God that it became easy for him to unleash God's power whenever it was needed. It looked easy and simple, and his followers were left aghast each time he said a simple prayer and things happened. Many did not realise how much time he had spent in agony before his father, how much he invested in communication with his father. He was so in touch with the source of power that he was able to release that power himself.

When we race against time, we need to keep in touch. We need to keep oiling the communication wheel. Prayer must be a lifestyle. We must not be caught napping as the three special disciples of Jesus did in his hour of need in the Garden of Gethsemane. This is an area that needs our constant, reflective assessment.

We must be intentional about our prayer journey. Whatever agenda we have for fulfilling our destiny, our requests must be known to God through prayer. Day in and day out, we must develop more of this habit, especially as we are aware that we are racing against time.

CHAPTER 9

Time to Serve More

But not so with you. Rather, let the greatest among
you become as the youngest, and the leader as one who
serves.

—Luke 22:26

Men and women of significance have been known for their
service. It is through their service that they were able to impact
many. Service is not a sign of weakness; it is a sign of strength.
It is when we use our skills and talents for the common good
that we catapult ourselves from ordinary to extraordinary.
Remember Mother Theresa, Mahatma Gandhi, and Nelson
Mandela. You don't have to be famous to make a difference
through service. Wherever you are, whatever talents you have,
this is enough.

What has God endowed you with? What can you do with
passion and zeal? Imagine you had only a few years to live.
Now is the time to serve God more through the things that
you can do well. In your church, at work, or wherever you

are, do it diligently and with gusto, knowing that your days are numbered and you only have twenty-four hours in the day. I am writing this book now because this is what I enjoy doing. This is my legacy, and when I am gone, many will continue reading the thoughts that God inspired me to write. If a single soul can be encouraged and motivated to serve more as a result, whether in China, Africa, or anywhere else in the world, I will be pleased. Surely there is something you can do well. Find it and package it throughout your days, months, and years. Do it consistently and reap the results of your efforts.

An old lady in far-flung Zimbabwe, Africa, found her passion in children's broadcasting. She did it over many years. Many children were inspired by her, and she continued well into her eighties. Listening to her over the radio was a joy, and that legacy remains. She served her community in this way and did it well.

Mother Theresa lived a life of giving and caring. She brought to life many who were on the brink. She did so lovingly because her passion was with the down-and-out of her community. She founded an organisation which is still helping the poor in the slums of India and across the world.

You may be doing something, but do more. We can never be satisfied with what we are doing. Some of the richest men and women on the planet are busy dishing out their cash towards worthy causes. Bill Gates has set his sights on eliminating malaria from Africa and other paths of the world. These people donate billions to worthy causes. You can do more for the neighbour on your street who may be struggling to make ends meet. The disabled lady who needs someone to talk to time and again. The children across the street who want to see someone demonstrating the love of Christ across the street. The jailed drug addict from across the road, whom you can visit in prison. Be someone in the neighbourhood who does not swear or gets mad out of impulse. You can serve your community more. You can do more at work.

Reflect on your skills for a moment. What are you good at? In what way have you utilised your skills for the common good? You hear people complain about the shoddy work done in church, stating that the pastor is not organised and the leaders have no clue what they are doing. In some cases, the people who criticise are themselves good administrators in their own right. They have failed to transfer their skills in order to impact the work of the church. In some case, it is because the leadership has failed to empower people to be able to use their skills.

Jesus came to seek and to serve those who were lost. He demonstrated this daily as he met men and women who were despised by the community. In the house of the Pharisee, Jesus served a woman of dodgy behaviour by allowing her to wipe his feet and pour perfume on his body. He invited a member of the revenue department to dine with him at his house, contrary to what the religious leaders thought.

He served in places where it was unheard of. He was

accused of mingling with sinners. He was a man of the people and did more to serve others. Barriers were broken. He had no chips on his shoulder. He even told of a parable where a man, after being beaten by robbers, was rescued by a foreigner and potential enemy.

When we serve, barriers are broken. We become concerned about people more than tradition and beliefs. In 2015, when Germany decided to take on up to a million Syrian, Iraqi and Afghani refugees, that was a demonstration of service. They wanted to do more for people who were in dire straits. What is it you can do more? Whatever we have not done by the time we pack our bags to leave the planet, it cannot be brought forward. It's the end, and everything is left here. Our ability to do more will lie dormant, never to be activated again.

This is the time to serve. This is the time to do more than we have done before. The cumulative effect of many of us doing our part to serve can change our world for the better. We become outward looking, keen to sieze any opportunities to do acts of kindness to others. In a world littered with selfish acts, we become selfless. Our homes cease to be castles, but open homes where we care for the unfortunate, where needs are met and lives changed. We can do more.

CHAPTER 10

Time to Mature More

Taking Responsibility for Your Actions

Taking responsibility is an important aspect of personal development. It's the urge to learn and continue to improve oneself in order to attain that status where you can be competent in whatever you do. As you learn, you change for the better, and you become a valuable asset to the community. Wine matures with years, and so does cheese. But it is what we put into our lives that determine who we will become.

In 1 Corinthians, Paul outlines the reasons why we must be mature. It is for stability, and it is for the corporate building of the body of Christ. It is so that we are not tossed to and fro by every wind of doctrine.

When you are racing against time, you want to be more than what you were in the previous year. You are striving to attain that goal for which God put you here on the earth. You want to attain it with excellence, and when you do so, you will influence many. You will grow others, and the sum total of you and others on the same path will enrich your community. For the church, it is so that we can be like Jesus, who is the model of excellence. He never did things half-heartedly but with precision, perfection, and passion. The more we individually strive for excellence, the more we will become stronger together, with no one lacking in competence.

The road to maturity starts with a plan. Just like in any personal development plan, you need to assess your skills and gifts. What things do you do best? Focus on these for the common good. The Bible starts from the premise that we all have talents, gifts, and skills. We are all able to do something, and recognition of what it is we are good at is the beginning of the road to maturity and personal development. It is a conscious effort to assess what you are made of, instead of aimlessly living without purpose. When you are racing against time, it must be focused living. Concentrate on the things that you do best and sharpen those skills. Have the flexibility to adapt and to learn new skills that help you manoeuvre through the maze of this complex existence that is our world today.

You want to be more than you were meant to be. You want to reach beyond the sky when it comes to learning and relearning. You want to be sharper than a two-edged sword. As iron sharpens iron, you want to be with those who can help you develop as you learn from them and they learn from you. Life becomes dynamic and action oriented.

Maturity therefore starts with knowing where you want to go, how you are going to get there, what skills you have, and what you would do when you find obstacles along your way. It is the ability to anticipate what might happen by planning for it before it happens. It is remaining focused no matter what. It is realising that seasons come and go, and that no one season can dominate the others seasons. What you need is to prepare for each season appropriately and slog on until it passes and move on to the other one. Mourning and whining will not change the basic laws of nature. It will instead deprive you of the opportunities each season brings, even in the midst of adversity. It is always smart to associate with those who think the same, who have the tenacity and the attitude to keep on keeping on.

When you mature more, you reflect more and are impulsive less. You are deliberate in the way you conduct your business. You want to learn more and criticise less. You appreciate more and complain and whine less. You are in control more and pander less to the whims of others. You are more assertive and less insular, and you have the confidence to meet your challenges head-on. In fact, you are in a good place.

I have found that the Bible is a great asset. It is a minefield of knowledge and wisdom to those who want to develop and become mature. It teaches, corrects, rebukes, guides, and fills the void in any life with the truth. David said, "Your Word is a lamp to my feet and a light to my path" (Ps. 119:105). In another passage, he says, "How sweet are your words to my taste, sweeter than honey to my mouth!" (Ps. 119:103). This is knowledge par excellence. Many laws, books, and the wisdom of the sages are steeped in the teachings of the Bible. It reveals the secrets of the heart. Here is what happened at Pentecost: "Now when they heard this they were cut to the heart, and said to Peter and the rest of the apostles, 'Brothers, what shall we do?'" (Acts 2:37 ESV). The word was so powerful that it demanded a response, as it always does. It transforms the hearer or the reader. You will never be the same, and that is personal development; that is maturity. We need more of this each day. It distinguishes between those who are mature and those who are not. The more you read, the more you are changed by what you read. You become exposed to new ideas, which in turn build you up into a new person. I have found that if you dovetail the reading of the scriptures with that of diverse literature, you enrich yourself and will never be the same again. It changes you.

You want to be a leader who is mature. A parent or spouse who is mature. A young man or woman who demonstrates maturity. The more you feed on those things that will help you develop to the next level, the better you are. Take the example of a leader who flouts with a young girl next door and all the time tries to hide this under the carpet. Or a politician who, over many years, has been a child molester or a lady in waiting trying to disrupt the course of justice using her position.

This is immaturity – the lack of a realisation that others have to be respected, a blatant flouting of those rules and regulations that have kept society together for ages. You see, if you don't change inside, you can't change outside. The more

CHAPTER 11

Time to Love More

> Love never ends. As for prophecies, they will pass away; as for tongues, they will cease; as for knowledge, it will pass away. (1 Cor. 13:8 ESV)

This is unconditional love. It's what the Greeks call agape love, a one-way type of love. It doesn't matter whether or not the other person accepts it; you still love anyway. Even when you are humiliated by the very person to whom you show love, you love anyway. This is the sort Jesus demonstrated on the cross of Calvary. When people deride, mocked, and spat at him, he still said, "Father forgive them, for they know not what they are doing."

This kind of love frees you. You don't carry any baggage. You are prepared to let go. Should the clock of life stop at any time, nothing will be in your in tray. You need more of this each day.

You can never love enough. You can never exhaust love. It keeps coming, seemingly oozing from the swelling ground of love which is God himself. God is love; he embodies it and he showers it. You flourish when you experience God's love. God loves us even when we are stuck in the slime of our sin. His love is unconditional.

There is nothing that love cannot do. There is no situation that love cannot overcome. That is why God's love is called agape love. First Corinthians 13 sums up this kind of love.

> Love is patient, love is kind. It does not envy, it does not boast, it is not proud. It does not dishonor others, it is not self-seeking, it is not easily angered, it keeps no record of wrongs. Love does not delight in evil but rejoices with the truth. It always protects, always trusts, always hopes, always perseveres. (1 Cor. 13:3–7 NIV)

We need more of this kind of love. We have not arrived yet. This is a commodity in abundance, but it's not utilised often. It neutralises the enemy, or rather disengages him. Love embraces the enemy and those who persecute you. What? Yes, love is so overwhelming that it is beyond pride. It does not think of itself but regards others as more highly than yourself. It is not concerned with what others think, say, or do, but it seeks to please God always. Love is not love until you give it away. It is to be consumed and not hoarded. You can't keep it in bundles, but it is effective when it is released into the atmosphere, when it is targeted at people.

We need more of this today. You must love more in order to impact more. You should love more in order to be effective more. You must love more if you are to grow more. Love transforms lives. It is dynamic, adaptable, and accommodating. We need to love more. Even if people don't respond to such love, we should love anyway – more so when we are racing against time.

The evidence that we love God comes when we love our brothers and sisters. John says,

> If we say we love God, but hate our brothers and sisters, we are liars. For people cannot love God whom they have not seen, if they do not love their brothers and sisters whom they have seen. (1 John 4:20 GNB)

Loving more means loving our brothers and sisters more, loving our enemies more, loving those who hate us more, and loving ourselves more. We were made in God's image, and therefore we are unique. We are of value not only to God but to ourselves. Many people take their lives because they give up. They think it is not worth it, but it is. If we love ourselves, we would not want to destroy ourselves.

In this competitive environment, sometimes we are not content with what we have, and we end up envying others' possessions. We become jealous, and we kill for it, we gossip about it. We hurt inside. Loving more is the opposite, for love is not selfish. Love seeks the good in others. Love promotes the other person. Love always sees the good in the other person, and it wounds for the benefit of the other person.

It is not just erotic, although this aspect of love has been promoted on social media and in films. It is much more than this. It is agape love.

Agape is selfless, sacrificial, unconditional love, the highest of the four types of love in the Bible. It stands out amongst the other types of love, like brotherly love, family love, and erotic love. It is forever and stands the test of time. We should have more of this. If the other types of love are underpinned by this love, our world would be a better place.

Jesus is our model of love. He taught, "You shall love the Lord your God with all your heart, and with all your soul and with all your strength and with all your mind, and you shall love your neighbor as yourself." (Luke 10:27) This love is both vertical and horizontal. Loving God gives you the power to love those you see. And because you acknowledge who God is and how he has loved you, you in turn are moved to do the same to those you interact with. In fact, such love is allergic to racism, prejudice, and discrimination! We need to love more, and all of us want to be loved more as well.

On reflection, are you loving more? Can you identify those who should be on the list to receive more of your love? Remember that we must use every opportunity because our days are numbered. Not only that, but enjoying this blessed life and loving more releases us to do just that. Target your family, your spouse, and your colleagues. Above all, love yourself. You are special. You are unique and were fearfully and wonderfully made by the creator. Go for it. Love more today and always.

This can only be possible if you love God with all your

heart, mind, and strength. He will give you the same love that he demonstrated when he decided to rescue mankind from sin. This is the love that can enable us love others.

The biggest challenge is to love your neighbour as yourself. This is a new definition of neighbour: someone whom you can sacrifice for, pray for, and do everything to help them. Jesus illustrates this by the parable of the Good Samaritan, a foreigner and an enemy who embraced his potential enemy and rescued him at the point of his need. What mattered was not the relationship but the need to help and be of service to the man. He ignored the enemy label on him and saw God's unique creation. He threw aside his reputation and what others would think of him. He risked all for the sake of his fellow human being. He saw more of what united them than what divided them. Many people have paid a great price for such love. This is what we are called to do as we race against time. Jesus raises the love standard to go beyond those in your camp. Now it includes enemies, outcasts, and those the world deems unacceptable.

Jesus says that it is not love when you love those who would love you back.

> But I tell you, love your enemies and pray for those who persecute you, that you may be children of your Father in heaven. He causes his sun to rise on the evil and the good, and sends rain on the righteous and the unrighteous. If you love those who love you, what reward will you get? Are not even the tax collectors doing that? And if you greet only your own people,

what are you doing more than others? Do not even pagans do that? Be perfect, therefore, as your heavenly Father is perfect. (Matt. 5:44–48 NIV)

This is a revolutionary type of love that knows no bounds. It's not reciprocal and is a one-way type of love. Jesus's analysis is spot-on. In the guise of culture, many of us are expecting to only greet those we know, not strangers. We expect to invite only those within our camp, the comfort-zone friends, those who will love us back. This is the norm, and everyone can do this. There is no challenge, no pressure, and no sacrifice. To love more means to go beyond the expected and to enter the realm of the possible, the uncomfortable zone, the unpredictable arena. It means loving those who do not love you and who may show disdain at you. It means greeting those who look like they are going to spit all over your face if you dare upset their routine. It means going against the grain of cultural and traditional etiquette. We need more of this as we race against time. There is a price to pay. Jesus has never minced his words. That is why he said to Paul, on the road to Damascus,

"Go!" said the Lord. "This man is My chosen instrument to carry My name before the Gentiles and their kings, and before the people of Israel. I will show him how much he must suffer for my name. (Acts 9:16 NIV)

Many people through the ages have suffered for showing more of this love that Jesus teaches about. We need more of this today, tomorrow, and always. Our leaders need more of this, not the hate exchanges that we see on television and read in newspapers. Not the tirades of anger and unforgiveness. Leaders must love more even when they disagree with each other. They must love more even when the chips are down and their backs are against the wall. What an example we learn from Jesus, when he was faced with the greatest crisis of his life. When chided and taunted while hanging on the cross, he loved more.

Reflect on areas where you need to do more of what Jesus taught. Reflect on areas where you struggle to love the unlovable, and on situations where your attitude has already been predetermined and you feel you can't love any more. We need to be deliberate and intentional, to make up our minds to do more and not do the same. We must show acts of mercy to those with whom society is fed up. It is hard, but it is the right thing to do. It is one more obstacle we must clear as we travel the road to our destiny. Go on, then. Do it now!

CHAPTER 12

It Is Time to Forgive More

Then Peter came to Jesus and asked, "Lord, how many
times shall I forgive my brother or sister who sins against
me? Up to seven times? Jesus answered, I tell you, not
seven times, but seventy seven times."

—Matthew 18:21–22 (NIV)

This is the ingredient that is desperately needed amongst
families, spouses, churches, nations. We need to do more. If you
have already forgiven the worst of your enemies, you need to
do more to the many others you still have an attitude towards.
The child whom you resent because of what she has done over
the years. The church leader whom you detest because he tends
to ignore you but appreciates other members. The boss who
for years has tended to pick on you for no valid reason. The
husband who has kept you prisoner all these years. The father
who molested you when you were a child. Whatever situation
you are experiencing or have experienced in the past, see if you
can forgive more. It's tough, but it is also therapeutic.

Jesus decided to forgive us even when we fell short of his

glory. When we were yet sinners, Christ died for us. He does not treat us as we deserve, because he knows we are but like the flower of the field. The bottom line is that because we have been forgiven, we have to reciprocate this magnanimous gesture from the creator of the universe. This is what he says.

> He made known his ways to Moses,
> his deeds to the people of Israel:
> The LORD is compassionate and gracious,
> slow to anger, abounding in love.
> He will not always accuse,
> nor will he harbor his anger forever;
> he does not treat us as our sins deserve
> or repay us according to our iniquities.
> For as high as the heavens are above the earth,
> so great is his love for those who fear him;
> as far as the east is from the west,
> so far has he removed our transgressions from us.
>
> (Ps. 103:7–12 NIV)

As God has forgiven us, we must forgive more too. What a difference this will make to our relationships. Healing will take place as we release the tension in ourselves, the anxiety, the stress, and some depressions that are a result of not forgiving others. It is hard work, but God enables us to go through this process. It is a must, and our choices are limited. It is for our own good and gives us freedom to concentrate on our personal development. We grow in abundance and are able to quickly transform our situations.

You don't want to arrive at your destination with your baggage full of unforgiveness. You don't want to be accused of harbouring thoughts that made it impossible for you to exploit your full potential. When you don't forgive more, you limit your ability to do more. You limit your creative potential and are not yourself. Something eats you from inside like gangrene. Release yourself from this prison. Feel free to fly like a bird and do those things that will edify you and build you into a person God wants you to become.

David forgave more, and that is why he sat at table with Saul's son Mephibosheth. Joseph forgave more and welcomed his brothers who had sold him to the Ishmaelites. Esau forgave more when he welcomed his brother Jacob, who had taken his inheritance. The father in the story of the Prodigal son forgave more when he welcomed his son, who had plundered his inheritance.

Above all, Jesus forgave more when he said to the thief hung with him on the cross that he would be with him in heaven. You have no excuse but to forgive more. If Jesus did it, why can't you? This is a great challenge today in our world. There is always a cry for revenge, and yet God urges us to forgive as he has forgiven us. We should forgive more because he has lavished us with his forgiveness in spite of what we have done and how we continue to live. This is a process, and it does not come easy. There is a price to pay. But Jesus paid the price too. He had to die so that we could live. He had to forsake heaven in order to ensure that we could attain our freedom. What a price to pay. What a love he demonstrated. We need more forgiveness today. This is a must. This is what God demands of us day in and day out. Will you take up that challenge? Will you forgive more? This is God's invitation to us today.

There are obstacles to forgiving more. You will not find many people supporting you to do this. Many will urge you to retaliate, and they will tell you that it is a sign of weakness, that you are being soft. "Act like a man," many will say. But this is not the stuff that oils forgiveness. Forgiveness embraces love and stops at nothing short of reconciliation. It has the ability to turn around situations.

Remember the elder son in the story of the Prodigal son? He resented what his father had done to the errant son, and he was jealous. Imagine what could have happened if the father had consulted him first before the younger son came home. These are the obstacles on the road to forgiveness. You get stuck unless you defy the odds and forgive anyway. Jesus was accused of supping with sinners in pubs when he extended his hand of fellowship. He did it anyway, and look what happened. The good news of Jesus Christ turned the world upside down and transformed people. Today, we are where we are because of forgiveness. You can change your situation when you choose to forgive.

Chapter 13

Time to Endure More than Ever

Keep on Keeping On

It is when you see the finishing line that it hurts more. You want to give in and feel you can go no further. It is when we are just about to break through the impasse in our lives that it seems it is tough, and we can't carry on. It is when we are about to experience the best that can be that we are distracted and then retreat. We give up and decide to quit. The rallying call on this journey is for you to endure more. to accelerate your pace of endurance, and to be determined to do all you can to reach the finishing line. It is a game of resilience, of determination, of keeping on keeping on. It is not for the squeamish, but for those who have courage and go for it.

When you are racing against time, you surely need to endure more. Jesus had twelve followers initially, but of these, only a few are mentioned after Jesus left them. It is possible that they gave up and went back to their original professions; the going was tough for them. Even when Jesus was alive, just before he was crucified, the disciples ran away because they could not stand the enemy. And yet, this was Jesus's final hour when he was about to complete the work of salvation for which he had come. At one occasion, he found them sleeping while he was in the midst of a confrontational prayer with his father. We sometimes think that life is merely a stroll in the park. It isn't. It is walking without fainting. It is not climbing from one mountaintop to the other. It is climbing up one mountain, descending that mountain, and climbing another.

When you are diagnosed with a terminal disease, it is not easy to endure more. When you are faced with death, it is hard to endure more. And yet endure you must. You need that inward resolve to continue hoping, trusting, and believing. Many did just that, and there was a turn-around in their lives. But for some, because their time was up, it didn't make a difference whether they endured. It's better to die while enduring then to give up as soon as the disease is flagged up. The man in the Gospel of John waited for thirty-eight years to be healed. He had almost given up because when Jesus tried to find out what he wanted, he gave him a lecture on how impossible it had been for him to break through. This can be the story of your life. You may have tried so hard for your breakthrough, to no avail.

Imagine someone who has not been married for years. He has seen friends and relations tie the knot, but not him. Word is going round in the family, community, and church, that he is having problems with finding a partner. Suddenly it gets into his head, and he is distraught and feels like it will never happen. Or consider parents with their only daughter, who has been brilliant and done well in her career but failed on the marriage front. In desperation, they have even tried matchmaking websites in an attempt to hit the jackpot. The message remains the same: endure more. The danger is that once such a defining decision is made out of desperation, the choice may be wrong, and this in turn will impact one's life forever. Someone has called it the permissive will of God – the desire to go against what God says because you think it is too late because you cannot wait.

Waiting for God can be frustrating and yet so fulfilling. It can feel as if you are being taken for a ride, and yet it bears long-lasting fruit. No wonder why there are so many divorces today. People rush into a decision about marriage without taking their time and seeking the will of God. Incompatibility sets in the moment they get married and because it was a thoughtless decision, and it flops. For some who decide to live together before marriage, the same happens because that is not the way God intended marriage to be. It is meant to be based on commitment, communication, transparency, and unconditional love. These are values that are timeless and beyond culture, and that have seen many a happy marriage flourish for years. Don't give up whatever you are faced with; keep looking to the future, keep hoping, and keep enduring. Remember that it is a race against time.

You may be struggling with an existing relationship. Be it a spouse, a child, or a parent. It has proved tough for years now. It may be that you have not been able to hold a sound conversation for a long time, and you are almost giving up. It is not worth pursuing, you say. You have sought counsel, but still nothing has changed. It is time that you decide to change, because unless you change, nothing will change. You could be right in the relationship but still examine areas where you can change. If it means demeaning yourself in an attempt to accommodate the other person, do it. It will make all the difference and will neutralise the other person. Others will realise their need to change as well. It is never easy and is an uphill battle, but all good things are an uphill battle. Be encouraged and change, and all else will change with you. Someone has said that life is not a bed of roses; it is the thorns that produce roses. Don't see the thorns in your life, but the roses. The thorns are there to facilitate a glorious life full of happiness and satisfaction. Whatever you are going through in your relationships, please concentrate on yourself. Do the best you can to improve yourself, and your influence can become a catalyst for new, meaningful relationships.

Endure means "to deal with or accept something which is not pleasant". You cannot shy away from your problem or challenge. Whatever it is must be faced head-on; you cannot pass on the buck. You are responsible, and you have to find ways and means to sort the problem. This makes us our own liberators, and that sometimes begs for skills to do it. Many people have been dependent on others, and when a problem arises and they cannot find the people dear to them who have helped them in the past, they crumble. Many have taken their lives because they have lost loved ones; they cannot cope any more. Enduring more means you take the bull by its horns and you are willing to stand. You must garner all the strength and resolve you have. In other words, deal with it. Life must go on whatever the circumstances. Sometimes things may fall apart, but that is not the end. A new day, a new beginning, will come. It always does. Summer cannot boast that it holds sway over the entire universe, because sooner or later winter will take its place.

So what is it that you are going through? How unpleasant is it? How does it compare with what the biblical hero Job went through? How did he deal with this tragedy? His response was, "Naked I came from my mother's womb, and naked I will depart. The Lord gave and the Lord has taken away; may the name of the Lord be praised" (Job 1:21 NIV). Wow! Did he struggle with what happened to him? Yes. Did he doubt? Yes. But he kept faith in the God who was responsible for his existence. He knew that however unpalatable his lot, God had not abandoned him; he was still in control. This response came out of an experience that had taught Job about who God was. You need this when disaster strikes. When word comes that your beloved ones have suddenly crushed on a plane and none has survived. When word comes from your doctor that you have a crippling disease that will see you paralysed for life.

Or when your husband or wife remains paralysed and unable to help himself or herself. You need to have knowledge of a God that far outweighs your immediate tragedy. You need strength – God's strength. Is it easy? No. But endurance means that you accept it and deal with it.

Take a moment to reflect on yourself, on the things that have dogged you for a long time, and on issues that have been difficult to deal with or to accept. The call is for you to accept what has happened and to find ways to overcome these obstacles. Then move on, because your present challenges will not be the last. They keep coming as all of us race against time – God's time. Before we finish the assignment God gave us when we arrived on planet earth, we will be called upon to endure more day in and day out.

There are many who have endured hardship at work, and going to work has become a drag. The job satisfaction has ceased to exist as many go through the motions to ensure that they have food on the table. They have stopped learning, and their value at work has not increased. This is the everyday challenge people face. But unless they change, nothing will change around them. Unless they deal with the challenge, no one will do so on their behalf. How do you endure more when you cannot get along with your boss? How can you endure more when your work mates have become so negative that you have no room to manoeuvre? Think of a strategy. Accept work as your contribution towards the assignment that God has given you here on earth. It's an assignment you must complete during your allocated time. Your attitude must change. You must find ways to bring value to your workplace, to be able to resolve relational issues that impede your progress towards the assignment God has given you. Remember that everything we do must be done to please he who brought us here in the first place: God.

Whether it is work or any venture, it is not done for your boss or your workmates, but for God. Anything that blocks your full realisation of your service to God should be resisted, and you should find ways to ameliorate it. It calls for your humility and recognition that those who seek to oppose you are in league with forces that do not want you to fulfil God's mission. Either you ignore them, or you make it obvious to them that all you care for is doing what God wants through your work and nothing else. Paul had the same attitude. He realised that in his work, fierce wolves would come to destroy what he had done. He continued to do what God had called him to do until he had accomplished his mission. That is the mindset that is required as we endure more in the face of difficult work struggles.

i

We can endure more because Jesus, who went before us, endured more. The men and women of faith who went before us endured more. Heroes of the faith endured more. It can be done because God has made available the resources to help us meet our challenges head-on. He wants us to stand and not buckle in the face of our adversities. He wants us to move on even when we have setbacks in our lives. As we have talked about before, there is a prize before us ready for the taking if we continue to be faithful. With God on our side, we can endure more. And if he is for us, we can endure. We can deal with our difficulties. Hallelujah!

Chapter 14

Time to Prioritize More

Making the most of every opportunity, for the days are evil.

—Ephesians 5:16 (NIV)

In a race, there are things that are of greater importance than others. These include exercise, discipline, focus, taking your coach seriously and watching what you eat. Ignore these and you are on the road to defeat and disappointment. It is the same as we race against time. Our focus must be on those programmes, activities and policies that will promote and make us realize our goals. This is where many people faulter. We ignore at our peril the master plan that has been put before us. This plan addresses the way we should live, how we must relate to others and what it takes to get to the final destination in the face of the many obstacles that are along the way. This calls for prioritisation, majoring on those things that matter.

Paul urges his readers not to live carelessly, but to understand what the will of God is. The one who brought you into existence expects you to live in accordance with his plan for your life. It is when you deviate from that course that you cease to live a life of meaningful existence.

If you have slackened, go back to the drawing board and concentrate on things that matter. Those things that have serious consequences if left undone, and you know the timescale. It won't be long before we leave here, so we all don't have time to waste. We are here for a season. What are the key areas of life that need our attention? One of the big questions is, "Where will you spend eternity?" Any reasonable person would want to keep issues concerning the next life as a priority.

What is required to prepare for that life? It's no good saying, "I don't believe in the afterlife." Surely it is a fact that we are all going to pack our bags and go somewhere, sometime, and for an eternity. That is a fact. Jesus was very clear about this. We are guaranteed a life of bliss in the future, on the condition that we forge a relationship with the creator of the universe through Jesus Christ. We are free, and God does not want us to go back to the yoke of slavery. Each day we must guard jealously the freedom and the life that Christ has given us. We must be vigilant and alert all the time. This means doing those things that will help us remain faithful before God – things that will not allow anything to sidetrack us. We need to keep striving, casting aside anything that does not help us achieve the objectives that we have set before us.

One of the obstacles highlighted in the Bible is the resurgence of Satan. He is referred to as a lion whose agenda is seeking anyone whom he can devour. He is described in 1 Corinthians as appearing like an angel of light. This means that he is cunning and shrewd, and he camouflages himself in order to waylay many who are set on the journey. How can we overcome such deliberate attempts to derail our mission? We must resist the devil. That's right: it is all about resistance, standing your ground and refusing to cower to anything that is thrown at you. There are many references in the Bible to standing firm and being steadfast. You plan your strategy even before anything happens. You anticipate the risk and manage it before it comes. You are deliberate about it, and you map your planned response to the attack.

This means that we need to prioritise more every day. We need to have a consistent programme of action if we are to be victorious at the end of the struggle. Paul says, "Put on the full armor of God, so that you can take your stand against the devil's schemes" (Eph. 6:11, NIV). The armour is taken before the evil day comes upon you. Paul outlines the armoury.

The word of God or the sword of the Spirit is key; it pierces the heart. It is active and powerful. Knowing and understanding it brings to us the confidence and the ability to withstand. The truth is equally important. Satan is called the father of lies, and if we attack him using the truth of God, he will be disabled and become functionally irrelevant. When we employ the truth, we are proclaiming Jesus. And because Jesus has defeated Satan on the cross, we know we are on the winning side. Yet the pressure is on every day to not tell the truth. We cannot pretend that we can win the battle with half truths, because that is what the world does. That should not be our strategy.

Chapter 15

Time to Not Procrastinate

Do it now! Do it now! Do it now!

Procrastination is the thief of investment. You want to do things when you want to do them and not delay. It is the ability to keep track of what is to be done at the time it should be done. Desires have been missed because of procrastination. Decisions have been botched because someone failed to do the little things at the right time. Being proactive is the opposite of procrastination. Jesus said he was on earth to do what his father had sent him to do. The emphasis was on doing, not milling around hoping to do yesterday's assignments tomorrow. It is planning for it and executing it at the appropriate time. It is a determination to do it whether or not you feel like doing it. It is the consistent fulfilling of the mandate given again and again. When Jesus says pray, you pray; when he says give, you give. You don't dally once the decision has been made.

When you set a daily task programme, you do the important things until you accomplish them. You don't postpone doing things and hope they will go away. When I set out to write this chapter, I lay in bed and knew I had to wake up at a certain time to do it. When the time came, thoughts raced through my mind. Should I do it now, or I should do it later? I was so comfortable in bed that I wanted a little slumber. What an attractive idea. But, thank God, I stood up, shoved away my duvet, went downstairs, had my devotions, switched on my computer, and started writing the first sentence.

We cannot pretend that doing it now is easy, but it *is* doable. This race is no ordinary race. We cannot postpone today's activities to tomorrow. Tomorrow is in a different time zone. What if tomorrow never comes? It is today that matters.

Time to Be Transparent More Often

> And no creature is hidden from his sight, but all are naked and exposed to the eyes of him to whom we must give account. (Heb. 4:13)

Who is fooling whom? You have nothing to hide when you are in the presence of God. He sees everything, knows everything, and can anticipate everything. The clearest example of this is in Hebrews 4:13, where the writer says, "Nothing in all creation is hidden from God's sight. Everything is uncovered and laid bare before the eyes of him to whom we must give account" (NIV). You cannot fool God, for he is the creator who knew you from your mother's womb. Nothing can be hidden. It's like a CCTV inserted in your body. This is the state of things, and knowing this has implications to your attitude towards how much of you should be transparent.

Adam and Eve were naked when they were created and lived on the planet. It never bothered them – until they did something of which God did not approve. As long as our conscience is clear and we are on course to doing what God wants, there is no problem. We are willing to share who we are and what we are all about to everyone. This is what it should be. It is when we want to hide something, when our closet stinks of forbidden stuff, that we become edgy and uncomfortable to share.

But this is folly. This is unsustainable because we shall one day account for everything that we have done in the body, whether good or bad. You see, we are all accountable to the one who created us, he who knew us from our mother's womb. He's the one who has guided our every step to where we are now. So what is the point of hiding? The Data Protection Act does not apply to him because he is the creator of the data, and he knows even unspoken things of life. There is no confidentiality clause with God, for he is the source of confidentiality. So be real and live in the open as you genuinely race towards your destiny, whether or not you are a leader. This is something that has eluded many leaders – living a life of intrigue, mystique, and self deception . Camouflaging oneself in the hope that the lie one lives will not come out in the open. The many leadership scandals bear testimony to this. Who in the end will be the leaders of tomorrow, as they take up the mantle and catapult this skewed world into something better for our habitation?

This remains one of the greatest challenges facing mankind. We may be technologically advanced, yet we lack the basic ethics of living that make who we are as human beings. It distinguishes us from the animal kingdom. We may be living in the twenty-first century, yet our morality is of the Middle Ages: uncouth, raw, and a free-for-all approach that lacks a strong moral fibre.

You as an individual are the cog in the wheel that can make the difference. It is as we personally develop our characters, our attitudes, and our moralities that we are able to influence others and thereby become part of the human revolution that, with God's grace, will build a strong society. We will be able to prepare this community for tomorrow and beyond. Even when we are not there, we can rest assured that we have done what God intended us to do and have contributed to our society. How can you make a difference? How transparent are you? What is in your inner closet that you are afraid of? How can you begin to untangle its hold on you and become transparent for the good of those you mentor and are responsible for?

Before we say a word, he knows about it. We are foolish if we think we can fool him at any time and escape unscathed. So why not succumb and live lives that are honest and transparent in our relationships with ourselves and wherever we are? Especially when we know that we are racing against time, we don't want to be caught napping; when the final whistle goes, we leave without settling the issues that have been hidden for ages. The husband and wife relationship demands openness and transparency; it is dynamic and developmental. Your goal is to be who you are supposed to be by undoing whom you are not supposed to be. This is no easy project, but it is a doable one. It begins with being naked with each other just as you do in the bedroom. You are not ashamed because you are one flesh. This needs to go deeper, to your thoughts, attitudes, feelings, opinions, struggles, and conflicts. It's no holds barred on any issue because the goal is to build the best relationship ever and influence the children the community and the nation. There is a price to pay when you are transparent in a relationship. You may initially feel odd and embarrassed, but in the long term you will be appreciated for who you are: a vulnerable human being saved by the grace of God. It is that vulnerability that becomes your strength in a relationship. You are approachable and easily corrected, and people never shy away from picking on your brain because they know that you are real and genuine. Like them, you are in need of encouragement and strength for day-to-day survival.

Transparency does not mean that everyone must know about what you do and who you are. It means that you must be transparent before God. He is your first port of call. When the going gets rough and you don't know what you do, you tell him. When there are issues that you have messed up, and you want restoration in your soul, you must tell him. It is equally important to have those close to you with whom you can openly share the innermost concerns of your life. As a leader, you need an inner circle in whom you can confide – people who will share your vulnerability and seek to cheer you on when you seem to stumble and fall. And for a pastor, the big question is, "Who is the pastor's pastor?" Many have fallen by the wayside because they have resisted revealing their innermost weaknesses to those close to them, they have sought to maintain a false sense of security and strength, and they have failed to maintain it when the going gets tough. The result is stories of pastors falling into sin, running away with girlfriends, and becoming suicidal and depressed.

We cannot maintain and sustain falsehood. It is not supposed to be so. There are so many ways that God has devised to help us go through this. If we are uncomfortable with sharing, then we can cry to God, telling him as it is. He listens, he cares, and he understands. Jesus said to his disciples, "My yoke is easy and light." He did not want his followers to unnecessarily suffer or bear a heavy burden. He was ready to help. In 1Peter 5:7 he says, "Casting all your anxieties on him, for he cares about you.". Casting means throwing whatever we have, and after that not looking back but trusting that God has resolved the issues. It does not mean we will not actively seek to practically resolve it. But as we do so, we are sure that someone is with us to help us. That matters greatly, and that assurance is key. But it begins with telling God what the problem is and actively engaging in the resolution of the problem. As Jesus says, "Ask and it will be given to you."

This is a critical skill. This is the beginning of resolving any issue, however big or small. And the asking must be intelligent. Be precise: how long, how big, and how deep the problem, and when you want it resolved. Give the extent of the problem and who is involved. Highlight some of the operational issues that have been a problem. That is what transparency requires: an openness on what it is that you want done and what it is you are finding it difficult to work around. This is being proactive. You are not firefighting but fire preventing.

Many young people go through these experiences on a regular basis. You may find it difficult to share with your parents that you have messed up. You may be afraid that this will result in you being ostracised. But should you decide to not share, the consequences will be graver, and the result will be detrimental to you and to those you love. The first step is to spill the beans to God himself; tell him about all your frustrations and what you want done. After you have done this, find someone to whom you can talk. And sometimes there are not many in whom you can confide. Ask God to show you someone, and he will show you. He will bring into your mind someone who can be of assistance. Then you will find that next time, you will be the one to help others go through their heart-wrenching problems. Any experience we go through is for a purpose, so when you stumble or fall, get up again. Be transparent, and you will reap the benefits.

Get Ready to Celebrate

Anticipation is the name of the game. You are in expectation mode every day and always. No athlete trains without expecting to win and to celebrate. They visualise this daily as their adrenalin kicks in, and they work hard for the day when they will stand on the podium, medal in hand, listening to their national anthem. It is a moment of joy, with tears trickling down the faces of brave men or women. For once, they succumb to emotion. This is the day, and this is the prize. The long wait is over. They have made it, and they are proud. Thousands pack the stadium and rise up as witnesses, spurring their heroes on.

As we race against time, we have a destination. We are goal oriented, and the prize is for the taking one day. When the celebratory mood kicks in from the start, it helps us to focus on where we are going. Obstacles and challenges fade and become hazy as we focus on the future and what we can achieve. Knowing where we are going and what we can expect when we get there becomes our inspiration. Everything else pales in insignificance.

How true. It is a long and winding road, but we will get there. This is the mindset of winners from the start. The prize overshadows what we might go through on the way.

Jesus summed this up on his final leg with his disciples: "But the one who stands firm to the end will be saved" (Matt. 24:13 NIV). At the final destination, we are assured of salvation, the restoration of our original image. In order to be able to get to that state, our today must be a celebration of tomorrow, today. This must be a constant reminder that where we are going is a result of what we are doing now. Our present will affect the future, and we need to keep upbeat about it regularly. We need constant reminders that we are going to celebrate finally when we have done our time here on earth. What we do every day should be a testimony that we are looking forward to celebrating in the end.

"I have fought the good fight, I have finished the race and I have kept the faith. Now there is in store for me the crown of righteousness, which the Lord, the righteous judge, will award to me on that and he goes on to say that a crown is waiting for him as a prize" (2 Tim. 4:7–8 NIV).

It is important that we know what we are going to celebrate, and not guess it. Such certainty will affect the way we do the business of the kingdom on earth. It gives us confidence and resolve because we know beyond reasonable doubt that that there is a reward waiting for us. Not only are we aware of what is ahead of us, but we are also aware of the criteria required to meet the requirements for that expectation. You don't just expect celebration if you have not met the requirements that God has stipulated in his word.

Your behaviour should reflect someone who is living in expectation off something grand on the horizon. You should live in accordance with your calling, not like people who have no hope. These people are careless with their lives because what they see now is it and nothing else. But for those whose allegiance is in Jesus Christ, their citizenship is in heaven, from where they await for a saviour who is Jesus Christ. This present is temporary and transient. What you do will be done in recognition that greater things are awaiting us one day.

Jesus told a story about a king who had invited special guests to a party. When many declined his invitation, he invited all and sundry who were able to attend. At the party, while people were celebrating, one was found to have come not dressed in the party attire expected of the guests. The host was not happy and ordered the person to be ejected from the party. The big lesson here is that there are expectations from the host of all those invited. There is certain etiquette, certain attire, and certain ways of doing things expected. You must be ready and must prepare. You have to do your homework. You can't simply gate crash at the last minute. We have all the time to do this. As we wait to celebrate, we need to know what we are celebrating and what is expected of us. Then we can go in with confidence.

The key is believing who Jesus is and what he has come to do. Embrace him as your new Lord and saviour. That is the first criteria. You cannot expect to celebrate at the party if you are not part of the woodwork. Part of those who have surrendered themselves unreservedly to the King of Kings and the Lord of Lords. You need to get things right with God before you can claim your seat at the banquet.

Commitment is number one. What follows naturally is living a life that pleases the host, Jesus. It means a daily walk in accordance with what he has instructed in the word of God. Your behaviour becomes different, and your speech mellows with the influence that comes from him. Paul says that "our speech must be seasoned with salt". It is not the careless talk that one hears in the marketplace among people who don't care a hoot about God's goodness. It is the science of living that respects your body as the temple of the Holy Spirit. You would not want to abuse yourself because you are made in the image of God. Out goes illicit sex, suggestive talk, pornography, and all other ills that are not pleasing to God. The good thing with the host is that he forgives. Should you want to repent and turn from the ways of the world that are not pleasing to him, he is willing to forgive. He wants to ensure that you won't miss the party because of the baggage that you are carrying. He is willing to offload the baggage for you, anytime and under any circumstance. What a host!

It is a celebration of God's love for mankind as God finally completes his plan of salvation. The guests are expected to live in love for God and for their fellow men. It is a party that will be steeped in the loving kindness of God. The sooner you practice it here, the better. It is one of the conditions of entrance to the great banquet. It is love not only for those you like, but also for your enemies. It is a revolutionary kind of love that Jesus taught. Not only are the guests expected to love, but they have peace that passes all understanding. This is God's peace and is not the kind the world offers. God's peace is enduring and lasting. It remains undisturbed even when the storm rages on unabated. It remains focused on the rock of salvation, Jesus Christ himself. All those preparing to celebrate have an inner peace, which only Jesus gives.

All the guests exude what the Bible calls the fruit of the Spirit. This includes love, joy, peace, goodness, gentleness, patience, joy, and faithfulness. These are the pillars supporting the character of the guests that are expected at the party. This

Chapter 16

Time to Give More Than Ever

> Give and it will be given to you. A good measure,
> pressed down, shaken together and running over, will
> be poured into your lap. For with the measure you use,
> it will be measured to you. (Luke 6:38 NIV)

God is the greatest giver, and he did it big time: he gave his son Jesus Christ. This is the greatest act of love ever made. You cannot out give God. That is why he challenges you to do more. You can never say you have given enough. The needs of men and women in the world continue to yearn for a helping hand. Many billionaire philanthropists have set goals regarding poverty alleviation and disease control, and yet the needs continue to increase unabated.

You don't need to be rich to give. You don't have to travel abroad to give. The needs are right on your doorstep, if only you open your eyes. Social media has made it possible for us to give more from the comfort of our homes. We are only a mobile phone away from tragedies in China, Japan, Somalia, and the farthest parts of the globe.

When we give, we make a difference. Love is not love until you give it away. Jesus gave an example of a woman who gave what seemed to be little, and yet she had given more. It cost her everything.

> And he looked up and saw the rich putting their gifts into the treasury, and He saw also a certain poor widow putting in two mites. So He said, "Truly I say to you that this poor widow has put more than all; for all these out of their abundance have put in offerings for God, but she out of her poverty put in all the livelihood that she had." (Luke 21:1–4 NKJV)

By writing this book, I am giving of my writing skills. I am sharing my passion with the world through you. I could have kept my thoughts to myself, but what good would that be? The joy of writing is that you occasionally hear people saying how much an idea in the book made a difference in their lives.

Imagine the billions of people across the world, each one with a passion a zeal for something. The cross-fertilisation of all the shared gifts and talents would transform our communities, nations, and the world. You have a part to play. The important thing is to realise how much what you give can impact others. You can give more than you have done before.

While Jesus was on the move, he was conscious of his mission. He had compassion for the lost, and at one time he looked at a mass of people and remarked, "They were like sheep without a shepherd." He identified where the need was, and he met that need. His business was not for selfish gains, but for the common good. He instilled this in his many followers. It can never be enough to sit on your laurels unless you do more for others. There is a therapeutic effect to giving more and doing more for others.

Jesus tells a story about people who were rewarded for doing much for others without realising it. When it came to the end of their race, those who gave more and those who did not bother to give were surprised:

> Then the righteous will answer him, "Lord, when did we see you hungry and feed you, or thirsty and give you something to drink? When did we see you a stranger and invite you in, or needing clothes and clothe you? When did we see you sick or in prison and go to visit you?"
> The King will reply, "Truly I tell you, whatever you did for one of the least of these brothers and sisters of mine, you did for me." (Matt. 25:37–40 NIV)

> They also will answer, "Lord, when did we see you hungry or thirsty or a stranger or needing clothes or sick or in prison, and did not help you?"
> He will reply, "Truly I tell you, whatever you did not do for one of the least of these, you did not do for me."
> Then they will go away to eternal punishment, but the righteous to eternal life. (Matt. 25:44–46 NIV)

It is the mere recognition that someone is in need and the act of giving that Jesus commends. He is not for the modern-day attitude, where we can sit and watch on our television screens starving children – and yet we enjoy it as news and do not do something about it. There is a lot to be said about philanthropists, people who have made it their passion to intervene in dire situations and assist. It may be paying fees for a poor girl or boy next door, or in some remote part of the world. That will make a difference to that person.

A story is told of a young boy whose parents were poor, but a missionary decided to help him. Today he is one of the most renowned ophthalmologists in Africa. Someone decided to do more, and the results were huge. It brings satisfaction to the giver and a lifetime of happiness to the receiver. The compound benefit is that the helped will probably do the same because of his or her experience. What stops us from doing what is best for our community and our world? As we race against time, giving more is an investment in our time and our resources. The benefits are huge, and there is a return to your investment through human capital development.

There is a story of the building of the temple in the Old Testament, where people flooded into the temple with their resources, gifts, and skills. In fact, God was so precise in the product he wanted that people with special skills had to offer their expertise. As the resources and skills came, the response was so overwhelming that there was no room for more. They had to close the door to any further contributions. They had given enough for the project. This is what the organisers said.

They went to Moses and reported, "The people have given more than enough materials to complete the job the LORD has commanded us to do!" (Exod. 36:5 NIV)

They not only gave, but they gave more than was required. This is a higher standard than that which is normally expected. This was a reflection of their maturity. They knew to whom they were giving: the King of Kings and the Lord of Lords. They could not outgive him, but they did their very best. This is when enough is not enough, and you do more and more. Wow!

CHAPTER 17

Time to Be Content and Worry No More

A brief self introspection will reveal the goodness of God to you. The fact that you live and move and have your being is enough evidence of the goodness and love of God. Many times we take life for granted until we experience real tragedy and see other people who are living worse lives. Job, following his devastating tragedy that saw his family perish within a short time, realised the importance of life itself. It became apparent to him that he had come into this world with nothing, and therefore he expected to take nothing back. He set his priorities in order. Losing his material possessions was painful but not important. He still had a God to depend on. Do you?

Paul, writing to his protégé Timothy, says, "For we brought nothing into the world, and we can take nothing out of it" (1 Tim. 6:7 NIV). What a sobering thought. The fact that we came into the world is a blessing. The material possessions are add-ons to our lives and are nothing to brag about. Such reflection is necessary as we live each day grateful for what

God has freely given us. It is he who deserves our praise and honour because of what he has done for us. David says in one song, "What shall I give to the Lord for all the good things he has done for me" (Ps. 116:12 NIV). How true. And the answer? Nothing!

Daily it is a matter of counting your blessings and focusing on the good things with which God continues to provide you. It's the basics: the air that you breathe, the family that you have, the job that is yours, the friends that surround you in times of hardships, the parents who have stood by you in your most vulnerable moments. It's also the people present and past who have been beacons in your life. The list goes on and on. Every one of us starts from a position of contentment for what God has done for us. And of course, Jesus says that eternal life is for the taking to all those who receive him and acknowledge him as the saviour. Hallelujah!

Contentment is an attitude of gratitude. It is the realisation and acknowledgement of those things that matter in life – things without which you cannot live or survive. The basics of life are just like the basics of the seasons. Winter, summer, spring, and autumn will always be there in full measure, whatever happens. They are guaranteed, and they make the world go round. You can't change that. And also with contentment, you are sure that God will always provide for the basics of life to all without favour. The poor man will always breathe the same air as the rich man. When that is not possible, they both die. Paul brings an interesting dimension to contentment. Contentment can be learnt. You can develop this attitude through experience.

Paul says, "I know what it is to be in need, and I know what it is to have plenty. I have learnt the secret of being content in any and every situation, whether well fed or hungry, whether living in plenty or in want"(Phil. 4:12 NIV). Paul had survived in many different situations. He realised that there was no need to lose sleep when the going was tough and when it was plain sailing. He was always able to come out of those situations with God's help. He had learnt, through bitter experiences at times, to remain constant and not panic. He continued to believe in a God who was a provider of all the things. I am sure there were times when Paul doubted whether he was going to make it, but he persisted and endured the pain and hurt, until he could proclaim publicly that he had what it took to be content with what God had given him. Amazing!

This attitude of contentment evaded the children of Israel on the journey to Canaan. No miracle or signs of God's intervention could help them learn this lesson. From the word go, following the miracle at the Red Sea, they complained, grumbled, and whined. They never learnt and remained where they were, unchanging, obstinate, and hard-hearted. The result? All of them above twenty years of age were refused permission to enter the Promised Land. You can almost hear God saying to himself, "I did all I could to provide for these people. "There was never a day that I did not demonstrate my

tented people enjoy the blessings of God. They are
nt on the one who is their sustainable resource base.
the in the goodness and faithfulness of God now and
They give God honour where honour is due, and they
in the habit of succumbing to constant rumbling and
g for no reason. Because they are contented, they always
ortunities to help those in need – the ones still struggling
atisfaction in the day-to-day worries of this world.

n you are contented, you are able to reign in anxiety.
rned his disciples against this when he said, "Therefore
e anxious, saying, 'What shall we eat?' or 'What shall
k?' or 'What shall we wear?' For the Gentiles seek
these things, and your heavenly Father knows that
them all. But seek first the kingdom of God and his
sness, and all these things will be added to you" (Matt.
NIV).

r as Jesus was concerned, anxiety is what those ignorant
God can do suffer from. What matters most is the ability
recedence to the creator and provider. Whatever we
l be taken care of. Anxiety is the direct opposite of
ent. It is the inability to take charge of yourself and
nder of your uttermost being to the elements, and not
Contentment means you shove whatever is bothering
e one who is able to keep you from falling. What is it
ents you from enjoying a life of contentment? What
ur anxiety package that cannot be chucked out into

power through great signs and wonders. And when they were in need, I provided them with food to eat, a balanced diet in the desert that was better than what their enemies fed on. What more could I have done to these people? But they did not change their attitude. They refused to learn contentment even though there was evidence for them to believe what I could do for them."

Contentment is a decision based on what has been before. You decide to be content because you realise that you cannot change your circumstances, but you can change yourself. It is the realisation that whether you grumble and mourn over a situation, ultimately you are responsible for what happens to you personally. You refuse to allow outside factors to influence the way you feel, especially the things that you cannot change. The children of Israel had never, in all their travels, effected change on anything. They were not responsible but looked to others to affect their lives. They failed to make a decision to live a life of contentment in spite of what was happening to them.

The decision to be content should be guarded jealously. It is when you are content that you are at your most productive. You are forward looking, you are responsible for your actions, you are accountable. People who are content reflect hope, faith, and a willingness to do the tasks at hand. They are infectious, bring others to their camp, and are great influencers. They have less stress and depression. They are great salespeople for the kingdom of God, and they attract their enemies and friends.

David did this, and so did Paul. So can you. Join the pack and decide to be content.

The decision to be content comes from reflecting on what God has done for you: the evidence of his trust, faithfulness, and continued provision of your needs. Sometimes it's the way he has rescued you from very difficult situations, or the way he has brought you to a better place after a loss, an abuse, or a situation where you were not to blame. The sum total of all these things that God has done and keeps doing brings us all to the decision that all is well. It is this hope built on the promises of God that remains unshaken. It is a realisation that there is in us the potential to weather the storms in our lives, however rough. Paul, the great philosopher and servant of Christ, demonstrated this throughout his life. He went through thick and thin, and yet he remained focused on Christ. He was confident in the God who delivered each time He was called on to do so. It was an unshakeable contentment. This is the stuff that makes up all those who are conscious of the fact that we are in a race against God's time.

When you are content, you hardly murmur. You refuse to blame others for the mess that you are in. You refuse to blame your parents, the government, your circumstances, and the weather. You take it upon yourself to resolve the issues. You become an instrument of peace and a solution, rather than the cog in the works. You don't stir up hatred and discontent, but like Jesus, you seek peace.

Your creative juices ooze because you have less stress. You are ready to the gifts and talents that God has give A decision to be content is transfor renewal of the mind. You will never

When you are content, you are le not impulsive, and you tend to be n others because of the realisation that the same God who has been so goo others and are willing to assist those come to the same state as you. You it does not come easy. There has to before you settle on a position of cont of the faith did this, and the story of what God can do to carve out co detests peace and serenity but al negatively to the rigours of life.

What prevents you from being drawing board, and in the words of

> Count your blessings name
> Count your blessings see wh
> Count your blessings name
> Count your many blessings
> And it will surprise you wh
> (Johnson Oatman, Jr.)

Con depende They ba forever. are not grumbli seek opp to find s

Whe Jesus wa do not b we drin after all you need righteou 6:31–32

As fa of what (to give need wil contentn the surre to God. you to th that prev is it in y

God's dustbin? It is not a recycling bin, but once it is there, it will never surface again.

You cease to worry when you realise that you cannot change a situation. When something is out of your control, you have no power to change it. For example, you fail an examination. Once the results are out, that is it – you can't do anything about it. You can cry, be depressed, or scream, but the result will remain the same. But if you decide to accept that it has happened and examine the reasons why you failed, you are on the road to recovery. If you encourage yourself and say, "I will be the best in this content matter that I have failed, because by doing it again, I will be more knowledgeable of the subject," that will make a difference, and your attitude will definitely change.

Worry blinds us from the opportunities staring us in the face. It denies us the creativity and the determination to meet our life's agenda and issues. It stunts our growth, and before we know it, it is too late. The secret weapon against worry is to keep going and never look back, to follow the example of ants. Even when ants are killed during their mission, they keep working. They are aware that if they don't, they will never accomplish their mission. There is no pity party. They realise that you cannot wind back the clock. When time slips from your grasp, it is gone, together with the opportunities. We cannot afford that as we race against time. Ants know it, and so should we!

Chapter 18

Time to Invest Wisely

It is ironic that many who are skilled in the things of this world lack wisdom in the basics of life. They ignore completely what Jesus warned about regarding this life and the life to come. Many are not prepared, and yet they brag when it comes to accumulation of riches, the pursuance of momentary pleasure, and the careless handling of what God has given. It is sad because though their skills can be useful in the kingdom, they have decided to ignore that and hold on to what they deem tangible. As a result, that which eventually leads to enjoyment of yet another experience is based on faith hope and love. What does one do to move from one experience to the other? That requires a sojourner mindset, a realisation that we are all in a race against God's time, and that we are here for a season. When the purpose for which we came is done, it is time to live another existence judged on what we would have achieved within the rules of living. It's simple and yet profound.

Jesus spent three years trying to drum up support for the kingdom. In fact, the Bible tries to present this narrative in a clear and concise way, but to the foolish, it does not make sense. Either we plod on blindfolded and refuse to acknowledge this revelation, or we diligently seek to understand the meaning of life and how this life can be lived and enjoyed to its fullest.

Although it makes business sense to invest, it also makes spiritual sense to invest in the things of the kingdom. The principles are similar. In the book of Hosea, God says to the people of Israel, "My people are destroyed for lack of knowledge" (Hos. 4:6 NIV). How true for both the business investor and the spiritual investor. When you become both a spiritual and business investor, this becomes a lethal combination to your benefit today, tomorrow, and forever. Sadly, many people don't get it.

You may be astute as a real estate investor, on the market, in stocks, or in any other lucrative investment. What matters is whether you are a smart investor when it comes to your life. The Bible is very clear and distinguishes between the wise and the foolish when it comes to the things of the kingdom of God. Either you are a wise man or a foolish man, a wise builder or a foolish builder, a wise girl or a foolish girl, a wise king or a foolish king.

Wisdom becomes important if we are to discern what is important and what is not. It is the principal thing. This is why many who are great in business fail to manage their own lives. Even some great car companies have ended up cheating the public for the sake of extra profits and a global reputation.

When they are caught, their foolishness is exposed. Some great CEOs have floundered and destroyed their families because they did not invest in wisdom. They were foolish.

When you are racing against time as we are, there is no time to fool around. Each moment spent must contribute to one's personal development. You should accumulate new knowledge – useful ideas that will enhance your life and make you prepared. It is not just working, but working smart.

Jesus was very practical. He was hands-on and could easily analyse situations and come to discerning conclusions. He contrasts people as either foolish or wise investors. As you go through these examples, reflect on which category you fit in.

Wise and Foolish Builders

> Therefore everyone who hears these words of mine and puts them into practice is like a wise man who built his house on the rock. The rain came down, the streams rose, and the winds blew and beat against that house; yet it did not fall, because it had its foundation on the rock. But everyone who hears these words of mine and does not put them into practice is like a foolish man who built his house on sand. The rain came down, the streams rose, and the winds blew and beat against that house, and it fell with a great crash. (Matt. 7:24–27 NIV)

The Foolish Man and the Wise Woman

The fool says in his heart, "There is no God."

They are corrupt, they do abominable deeds;

there is none who does good.

The LORD looks down from heaven on the children of man,

to see if there are any who understand,[a]

who seek after God.

They have all turned aside; together they have become corrupt;

there is none who does good,

not even one.

Have they no knowledge, all the evildoers

who eat up my people as they eat bread

and do not call upon the LORD?

(Ps. 14:1–4)

"The wise woman builds her house, but with her own hands the foolish one tears hers down" (Prov. 14:1 NIV).

The Bible is a book of contrasts. It talks of the foolish man and a wise man. The foolish man says there is no God. He does not acknowledge the existence of a world fashioned by a great designer. He assumes that everything just came into being, unaccountable. He cares for himself and does what he wants.

On the other hand, the wise man seeks wisdom. Like Solomon, he acknowledges who God is. He appreciates his existence and is accountable to God the Creator. The wise man or woman recognises that we are all accountable, that we have a responsibility towards the creator: to fear and obey him. We are not rolling stones that gather no moss. We are not zombies that jaywalk aimlessly and uncontrollably without direction. We have a beginning and an end, and what we do in between is important. We purposefully work to fulfil our mission. That is our reason for being here.

We invest in the things of God. We plan, we act, and we focus on what God set as our agenda for the time we are in this world. That is being wise. That is being purposeful.

The Wise and Foolish Son

The wise and foolish sons display contrasting characteristics. They seem to live in two different worlds. Proverbs gives an account of a foolish young man. He does not care about anything, makes foolish decisions, and is easily distracted. He is sensuous and is led away by erotic women who are interested more in his body than in his personality. He is easily exploited and manipulated, and he ends up shameful, broken, and without integrity.

> With persuasive words she led him astray;
> she seduced him with her smooth talk.
> All at once he followed her
> like an ox going to the slaughter,
> like a deer stepping into a noose

till an arrow pierces his liver,
like a bird darting into a snare,
little knowing it will cost him his life.
Now then, my sons, listen to me;
pay attention to what I say.
Do not let your heart turn to her ways
or stray into her paths.
Many are the victims she has brought down;
her slain are a mighty throng.
Her house is a highway to the grave,
leading down to the chambers of death.

(Prov. 7:21–27 NIV)

What a tragedy. This is what foolish sons do, and the world is full of them. You can remove yourself from this category. You can be streetwise and obey what God says and be safe.

On the other end of the spectrum, this is what a wise son does and what God expects.

Listen, my son, to your father's instruction and do not forsake your mother's teaching. They are a garland to grace your head and a chain to adorn your neck. My son, if sinful men entice you, do not give in to them. (Prov. 1:8–10 NIV)

Wise and Foolish Kings and Queens

God gave Solomon wisdom and very great insight, and a breadth of understanding as measureless as the sand on the seashore. Solomon's wisdom was greater than the wisdom of all the people of the East, and greater than all the wisdom of Egypt. He was wiser than anyone else, including Ethan the Ezrahite – wiser than Heman, Kalkol and Darda, the sons of Mahol. And his fame spread to all the surrounding nations. (1 Kings 4:29–31 NIV)

One would expect that royalty means wiser and smarter. Not so. Over the ages, there have been very foolish kings and queens who have failed to make the mark when it came to investing into the kingdom. Today, it is still the same. Kings and queens and princes and princesses took the wrong decisions, messed up, and ended up without honour.

Nebuchadnezzar was one of the greatest kings who ruled Babylon during the time of Daniel. He was prosperous and had everything. But he was proud, was full of himself, and did not acknowledge God. Here is one example of his foolishness.

But when his heart became arrogant and hardened with pride, he was deposed from his royal throne and stripped of his glory. He was driven away from people and given the mind of an animal; he lived with the wild donkeys and ate grass like the ox; and his body was drenched with the dew of heaven, until he acknowledged that the Most High God is sovereign over all kingdoms on earth and sets over them anyone he wishes. (Dan. 5:20–21 NIV)

shied away from them. They were uncomfortable and did not make the grade. They preferred staying in their comfort zones.

Opportunities are like seasons: they come and go, and they will come again. The key is to stay alert and seize them defiantly when their season comes. In a race against time, this requires a daring attitude and aggressive proactivity. There's a willingness to learn the hows of taking opportunities. When you think of it, it is not difficult to do this.

How can you love more, for example? How can you forgive more? How can you serve more? Jesus revolutionised all these acts of kindness. He loved his enemies. You love the unloved, and you pray for the unprayed. Your attitude towards those you detest goes through osmosis. There has to be a paradigm shift in your mind. It is now an opportunity for reverse thinking. The unloved become the loved, and the unforgivable become the forgivable. You are now operating in the end zone where every opportunity must be used to create new ways of doing kingdom business.

It is not the time to play games, hold grudges, or waste on tissues and not issues. It is a time to communicate wisely, to talk worthily, and to serve others with the love only God gives.

Follow God's example, therefore, as dearly loved children and walk in the way of love, just as Christ loved us and gave himself up for us as a fragrant offering and sacrifice to God.

But among you there must not be even a hint of sexual immorality, or of any kind of impurity, or of greed, because these are improper for God's holy people. Nor should there be obscenity, foolish talk or coarse joking, which are out of place, but rather thanksgiving. For of this you can be sure: No immoral, impure or greedy person – such a person is an idolater – has any inheritance in the kingdom of Christ and of God. Let no one deceive you with empty words, for because of such things God's wrath comes on those who are disobedient. Therefore do not be partners with them.

For you were once darkness, but now you are light in the Lord. Live as children of light (for the fruit of the light consists in all goodness, righteousness and truth) and find out what pleases the Lord. Have nothing to do with the fruitless deeds of darkness, but rather expose them. It is shameful even to mention what the disobedient do in secret. But everything exposed by the light becomes visible – and everything that is illuminated becomes a light. (Eph. 5:1-13 NIV)

Such behaviour is universal, and it has consequences. It is retrogressive and does not edify. It is not a proper investment of one's energy, time, and ability. It is amazing that even on television, there is a *blip* sound whenever there is inappropriate language.

We all can find opportunities to do more than what we

are doing now. We can love more, make it our desire to make a difference wherever we are, make use of the time we have to deliberately target candidates for our love, and proactively do something. Cut their grass, do the shopping, smile more, and cuddle more. Do anything that will make neighbours quip and exude appreciation within themselves. Do anything to make someone with a terminal illness see hope, rekindling faith in the God who heals and comforts. This is what we are here for. This is how we should spend our time doing. There will never be enough of it, so go on and do it today, tomorrow, and always.

CHAPTER 19

Be a Winner

I fought the good fight, I have finished the race, I have
kept the faith.

—2 Timothy 4:7

You start a winner, and you end up one as well. That was what
Jesus did. John the Baptist, who baptised him, immediately
recognised who he was. It was evident from the start that the
two were not cut from the same cloth; they had different roles
to play. John pointed the world to the coming of Jesus, and
Jesus was the real thing. He was God incarnate on a mission
to restore the broken relationship between man and God. He
knew, he never doubted, and he acted accordingly.

Unfortunately, many of us take years – and sometimes a
lifetime – to discover our purpose and resuscitate the mindset
of a winner. That affects your agenda on this planet. It
influences the way you talk, walk, and do business. You are
never apologetic about the life that God gave you freely. Each
day, however dull, ignites a ray of hope and inspires you to do
that which you were meant to do to accomplish your purpose.

It may be a small step towards your goal, but it adds up, and soon you are on the road to achieving your life's goals.

Be a winner in your mind. If you don't win the battle of the mind, you will lose the battle outright. The mind is where the war is won and lost. We ought to transform our minds. Once the mind is transformed to think Godward, the devil cannot make it his citadel and cannot direct his operations from that complex seat of our will and emotions. If you win there, you win everywhere. It is where you are able consciously to throw the arsenal towards the principalities and powers that daily ravage the borders and territories surrounding your physical make-up.

Are you a winner in your mind? Are you able to hold captive the destructive thoughts that come flooding into your mind every day? Paul says, "We pull down every proud obstacle that is raised against the knowledge of God; we take every thought captive and make it obey Christ" (2 Cor. 10:5 NIV).

It is possible to reign in any thoughts that come through the mind. We have the power through Christ to do it. We can win on this front because we are not alone; we are armed with the whole armour of God. Each day, we plan our line of attack and defence. We guard against anything that wants to take you captive or wants to influence our thinking and seek to disable and discourage us. We need to win in our minds if we are to win in our lives.

It is important to feed the mind with those things that will help to ward off any attack. David the king discovered this many years ago. David was proactive and prevented the attacks before they came. He took action to prepare for the evil day. That was what Jesus did in the desert when he was confronted by Satan. He responded to Satan's luring by quoting the scriptures. For every attack by Satan, Jesus had a ready response. Imagine if Jesus had not prepared. It would be easy to succumb to the devil's machinations and schemes. Armies across the world keep training and preparing, even in peacetime. The reason? When war suddenly erupts, they are able to respond with precision because they are ready.

We need to keep preparing, keep training, and keep anticipating what is to come. We are in it for the long haul. It is not going to end until we complete our race; it is a lifelong occupation. If we slacken and lose the winning mentality, we become easy fodder for the devil. Losing is not an option – you are in it to win it!

Whoever you are and whatever you do, you endeavour to excel. You shun mediocrity, the attempt to use a spoon instead of a shovel. You go for the very best. This becomes infectious and impacts those with whom you come into contact. You make a difference and influence others. You are constantly developing yourself in order to bring the very best in you. In order for things to change, you've got to change.

Peter could only change his world when he changed himself though God's power. He became a winner. He was bold and willing to take the authorities head-on for the sake of the good news about Jesus Christ. He became the champion of the downtrodden, the Gentiles. He ended up in jail and faced opposition all his life. Being a winner is risky, but that is the stuff that followers of Christ are made of. In fact, the winning attitude should be in every one of us.

Manage yourself. Unless you put your body, your physical self under subjection, your road to success will be littered with setbacks of all kinds. You don't win on just one front but on all fronts. It is a holistic kind of winning. If you are a family person, how are you winning on the home front? Is your home brand solid, or is it helter skelter? If you cannot manage your two or three children as a CEO of your family, then you have lost control. Team Family is your immediate family. It is how you manage it that will affect how you manage others outside the home. Any decisions you make have a bearing on the family you lead. You have to reflect and prayerfully think of what you are doing. You cannot afford to sleep at the wheel. You are in charge. Unless you are able to manage your family, you cannot count yourself a winner.

The world is full of derelict parents who on the surface appear polished and organised and who inwardly demonstrate shoddy characters. You are not one of these – you are better than that. You must walk the talk. You must be genuine and not fake. You cannot afford to be otherwise, especially as you race against time. Character matters. Integrity matters. When you live an exemplary life, you can pass on the baton to your children with pride and gusto, satisfied that you have done your best.

Winners demonstrate this not only through their subjugation of the mind, but also through their leadership of Team Family.

Be a winner in your marriage. It's no good being loving when you struggle to win in your relationship with your spouse. I am learning too. Marriage has been God's greatest design for mankind. When he proclaimed the two shall become one flesh, he revolutionised the relationship between man and woman. Two people, coming from divergent backgrounds and becoming soul mates forever, can only be something that God facilitates. It is not for a season, or for when things are well but forever. In sickness and in health, for poorer or for richer, until death do us part – wow! The greatest minds have failed to comprehend this. Some of the richest people in the world have struggled to live such a life. It has eluded many young men and women, as well as the most creative writers and thinkers. For every five people who marry, at least half end up in divorce. This means fewer winners and more losers.

Paul tells Timothy that for people to become a leader in the church, they have to be able to manage their families and be one husband for one wife. You cannot manage other relationships if you have failed to manage your own. Sadly, this has happened and is still happening. People in key positions of leadership have messed up in the home with their husbands or wives but are still clamouring to have an impact outside. God desires that we sort ourselves first and then be of service to others. Are you a winner in your relationship? Paul lays out the key requirements for marriages to succeed. He outlines the different roles each partner has to play in order for the synergy between the two to take place. Here is the deal.

Wives, submit to your own husbands, as to the Lord. For the husband is the head of the wife even as Christ is the head of the church, his body, and is himself its Savior. Now as the church submits to Christ, so also wives should submit in everything to their husbands.

Husbands, love your wives, as Christ loved the church and gave himself up for her, that he might sanctify her, having cleansed her by the washing of water with the word, so that he might present the church to himself in splendor, without spot or wrinkle or any such thing, that she might be holy and without blemish. In the same way husbands should love their wives as their own bodies. He who loves his wife loves himself. For no one ever hated his own flesh, but nourishes and cherishes it, just as Christ does the church, because we are members of his body. "Therefore a man shall leave his father and mother and hold fast to his wife, and the two shall become one flesh." This mystery is profound, and I am saying that it refers to Christ and the church. However, let each one of you love his wife as himself, and let the wife see that she respects her husband. (Eph. 5:22–33 NIV)

Husbands are called upon to love their wives as Christ loved the church and died for her. This is no ordinary love – it is Christ-like love, the love that he showed by dying on the cross for the sins of the world. This is agape love, unconditional love, sacrificial love. It's a love that never lets you go and that is not dependent on being loved back. Got it?

Sadly, there are wives who have become prisoners and are abused by "Christian" men. Men also have become willing slaves in homes where they cannot dare raise their heads. That is not winning.

You can only win in your marriage when God's love is demonstrated. It is not seasonal; it remains constant, come winter, spring, or autumn. It is not as fickle as the weather. It is God's kind of love. Joseph was engaged to Mary, the mother of Jesus. When he found out she was pregnant, he secretly thought of divorcing her, not wanting to expose her. It was not his pregnancy. He could have shouted from the mountaintop, but because of his love, he did not. This love does not expose – it protects. That's God's love. That is what we do when we want to be winners in our marriages. Sadly, that is not the way many approach this. Tabloids are full of marriage partners in church and outside it who have exposed their relationships for public consumption. Are you a winner in your relationship? Then take a cue from what Paul says.

To be a winner, you must fulfil your role of submitting to your husband just like you would to Jesus, the author and finisher of your faith. The husband ceases to be an ordinary block you tied the knot to; he takes on a new meaning. He represents the Godhead, Christ himself. You are doing this as unto the Lord, to whom you are accountable when your days are done here on earth. It makes such a relationship unique. It transforms our attitude towards the person we are to live with for the rest of our lives. Also, the husband should love his wife as Christ loved the church. Both are doing it not for themselves, but for the Lord. It is not a selfish kind of relationship, but one immersed in the Godhead. No wonder it is meant to last forever. No wonder many distractors want to destroy this institution that reflects God and not man. Sadly, many men and women have reneged on this contract. They have neglected what God wanted marriage to become.

Be a winner in your marriage, and it will be easier to win outside in the community, at work, and wherever you go. Fear God in your marriage and do what he tells you, and you will fear God elsewhere. This will impact nations and make God the creator and the authority he is. Righteousness exalts a nation, and it starts in your marriage, between two people. Then it ricochets into the community and nation. It becomes a blessing and not a curse. It can go viral. You children and your children's children will live under this tradition for generations to come. Come be a winner in your marriage and all relationships.

Are you battling with the question "Who will marry me?" It is one of the most difficult decisions one can make in one's life. Your shopping list has to be carefully drafted, and the items have to be carefully considered and chosen in accordance with what God wants. Whoever is going to marry you has to put on the agenda, the requirements of this important decision – the qualities, the qualifications, and the challenges of such a relationship. They have to subscribe to the same code of conduct as you and be committed to following Jesus and what he says. This is why the Bible says, " Do not be unequally yoked with unbelievers. For what partnership has righteousness with lawlessness? Or what fellowship has light with darkness?" (2 Corinthians 6:14) This is not discrimination, but a realisation that it is impossible to match two people who are driven by different sets of values and expect them to blend. Unfortunately, many people have defied this basic principle and gone for such relationships. The result is that there are cogs in the wheel, and the chariot gets stuck in the quagmire of incompatibility. Sad. Instead of asking, "Who will marry me?" maybe ask yourself, "Am I someone who will attract those who love Christ and live by his commandments?" You attract what you have become. If you seek to live a life that pleases God and are keen to follow him, many of like mind and orientation will be attracted to you. When you are in relationship, seek to live by what God says, and you will be a winner when you finally become one flesh.

Be a winner in your interpersonal relationship with God. Men and women of God who became winners had an encounter with God. They conversed with him regularly and were accountable. They sought to do what he told them daily, and through this they were able to accomplish lots in their lives. Daniel had a lifestyle of prayer, constantly touching base with the creator of the universe and getting instructions from him. Annah in the New Testament made it her occupation to live in the temple and to pray and fast for the rest of her life. Jesus set the example when he prayed early in the morning and throughout the night as he sought to do what his father had appointed him to do. It is winning on this front that has kept men and women of God on the winning side. Struggles come, but they have overcome them through a deliberate strategy to talk to God when the going gets tough and they are unable to cope. When Jesus was in Gethsemane praying, the disciples faltered and ended up running away when the enemy sought to kill Jesus.

What a difference when, after 120 of them prayed in the upper room, the Holy Spirit fell; they were not the same again. In 1 Timothy, Paul likens followers of Jesus as soldiers: they take their commands from him and remain faithful to the commander in chief. To whom are you faithful? Get real and hook up with the King of Kings and the Lord of Lords.

CHAPTER 20

Equip Yourself

Some years ago, I heard a story of a young girl who complained to her granny that she hardly ever got noticed by boys, and therefore she was upset that she might end up not getting married. The granny smiled. When she told granny that she had just finished her first degree, she was told to do a master's. Years later when she finished, her granny asked whether she was getting married. She still had not found a husband. She told her to do a PhD. You see, the granny was saying, "Don't worry about not getting married. But while you wait, equip yourself do something worthwhile." It is this preparation that sets you off to greater things, and whenever you get what you want, you will be prepared to play your role. It is competence that matter. Expertise comes with training and long hours of doing the same thing again and again.

We alluded to the lives of Jesus and John the Baptist in earlier chapters. They spent years in the wilderness, out of the public's view. Were they sitting idly by? No, they were being prepared for something greater. When the opportunity came, they hit the ground running because they were equipped. They knew what they were doing because they had practised this for a long time. Remember Moses, that great leader of the Jews? He spent forty years in the palace and forty years in the desert. When God gave him the responsibility to lead the Jews from Egypt, he was eighty years old, but he was well equipped and prepared for the task ahead. Those years were not wasted but came in handy when he was called upon to lead.

Few Bible characters are better known than Moses. The familiar stories of his rescue by Pharaoh's daughter, the burning bush incident, the ten plagues, the parting of the Red Sea, and receiving of the Ten Commandments are taught to children at the earliest ages in virtually every Jewish home. He has been immortalized in the hall of faith in Hebrews 11. Moses is emphasized throughout Old Testament scriptures as the model prophet of God. Many readers of the Bible lift characters up on pedestals, thinking that these men and women were divinely gifted at birth to be superhuman. Moses's life demonstrates how Yahweh, the God of Israel, used an ordinary man to accomplish his purposes. Moses was born into a Jewish family during the years of slavery in Egypt. His father was Amram, and the name of his mother was Jochebed. Aaron was his elder brother, and Miriam was his elder sister. The Bible describes nothing of his childhood and adolescent years, except for the fact that he grew up in the home of Pharaoh's daughter, where he became her adopted son. His membership in the royal family provided him the best possible learning and growing opportunities of the ancient world. After fleeing to the Midian wilderness following his act of murder, he met and married his wife, Zipporah. They had at least two children, Gershom and Eliezer.

How did God equip Moses in the first forty years? He rubbed shoulders with royalty. He must have received training from the very best because he was regarded as a prince in Pharaoh's household. What is your passion? What are you good at? Hone your skills. Personal development is one of the greatest assets one can ever have. Work at yourself, continue to learn, be inquisitive, and read. It will make a difference to your life. You will be racing against time fully equipped and confident that you are doing the right thing.

I am reminded of what happened to me years ago while working as a curriculum designer, writing syllabi and materials for schools. I used to write poetry and always kept a folder with different drafts. There was a World Aids Day, focusing on women. Naturally I wrote a poem and kept it in my folder. Months later, it came to my attention that UNICEF had commissioned our department to write HIV/AIDS materials for schools. Unfortunately, the team had already been selected. I was not invited to join the team.

One morning I bumped into the coordinator, and I expressed surprise that the team was already in place and I was not in it. I then jokingly said, "It's a pity because I have written a powerful poem on HIV, which you could have used for your materials development!" That was the tipping point. She wanted to have a look at the poem, and I ended up being one of the team leaders. You see, I had prepared myself. I was equipped, and my skill that I had developed gave me the opportunity to be part of a creative team that developed unique materials that were used throughout the country.

Are you readying yourself every day? Whether through reading, interaction, training, or doing a course of study that will prepare you for the tasks ahead, waiting is strategic. While you wait, you ought to do something. In a race against time, the more we develop ourselves, the more we will live a meaningful life that will impact others around us. We can become people of influence because wherever we are, we will exude confidence, technical competence, and skill.

The days of landing a steady job with a predictable workload are over. The problem for today's organisations is that few, if any, of them can predict what challenges they'll be facing in a year's time. This is actually good news for individuals.

One thing is certain: in our uncertain world, organisations will have to become more agile and more responsive to macro trends and factors beyond their control. Their success will depend to a large extent on whether they can recruit and develop employees who have the capability and capacity to work effectively and take advantage of opportunities that arise. In other words, they'll be looking for people who are talented, resilient, adaptable, imaginative, and trustworthy. These five traits, which form the acronym TRAIT, are the key skills that you need to highlight on your CV. You'll also need to show that you have a positive mindset because that will impact on whatever job you're asked to do.

Ignorant people will always flout and flounder. They lack confidence and find it difficult to mix with others at a professional level. When you race against time, you must be knowledgeable about yourself, the future, and the creator of the universe. You need to know where you are going and what you need to do in order to get where you are going. This must be a regular reminder so that you are not caught unawares when the time comes, and your clock decides to lose steam and packs you away.

Reading is one of the best forms of acquiring knowledge. Imagine: if you read two books every week, you will have read a hundred books by the end of the year. You will never be the same again. Your attitudes will change, your response to life's challenges will be altered, and you will generally live a better life. I have found reading therapeutic. It resolves many issues and makes you want more of the insights of men and women who are creative and willing to share their thoughts and feelings with the world.

Jesus rebuked the religious leaders of his day for not knowing the scriptures. They lacked understanding of what God had said, and that affected their attitudes. When you are informed, you have very little time for unnecessary things, foolish controversies, and other mindless hiccups. You concentrate and meditate on what you read. You are always reflective as you chew the cud on the things that you will have learned. This becomes your skills base as you are able to plan your strategy from a position of knowledge and understanding.

CHAPTER 21

Be an Example

Jesus walked the walk and led by example. When one day you will be no more, people should look back at your track record and be grateful that you ever lived. Paul could easily say, "Imitate me." Now, that is a stinger. He knew where he stood and what he did, and he was not ashamed. We ought to be men and women of integrity, ready to be believed whenever we do stuff. While the world is slowly degenerating into a circus full of fakes who mask their faces, we are different.

Our reason for being is to honour and worship God, and to let people see a bit of him in us. We are made in the image of God, and that in itself has implications on the way we conduct ourselves during the time we are on this beautiful planet. We are a reflection of the creator of the universe, and it is his presence we must exude all the time. Paul says, "You are not your own, you were bought with a price." It is that realisation that makes us unique. We don't just survive – we live on purpose, and each day we reflect the glory of God. Because God is present with us every day, the life we live must reflect that reality.

If you are a follower of Christ, you are the temple of the Holy Spirit. That is massive! You house part of the deity. In fact, Jesus goes on further, speaking to his disciples just before he physically left earth.

> Jesus replied, Anyone who loves me will obey my teaching. My Father will love them, and we will come to them and make our home with them. (John 14:23 NIV)

You don't want to live a mediocre life when you are racing against time. You want to demonstrate the characteristics of God through your life. The result? Many will want to follow your example at home, at work, and wherever you find an opportunity to interact with people. Remember Jesus. To many, he was simply the boy next door, a carpenter's son, but he was different. He reflected God in his life every day. He socialised with the outcasts, healed the sick, and went to places that were religiously questionable. He met women of dodgy character, but his reputation remained intact. He was a man of integrity. Compare him with the religious leaders of the day, pompous and dazzling from the outside, but shallow on substance inside. He once called them white-washed tombs with dead bones inside. Their impact? Nil.

This is the lifestyle of people who are conscious that they are racing against God's time. Your character becomes a treasured possession, and you guard it jealously. You make every effort to protect it. When David had sexual intercourse with Uriah's wife and was told point blank that it was wrong, he confessed and repented. He realised that it was folly to keep on living a lie and not asking the one who lives in him to forgive him. When he did so, he impacted his world. God said about him, "A man after God's own heart." We need a plan for our character before a plan for impacting the world. Sadly, many people treat serving God as something academic and not affecting their moral character. It is not so. God lives in us, and he is a holy God who demands that we live in accordance with what he says.

If you are a parent, your example should begin at home. Your children must be able to emulate your character. The God in you must be evident in the manner you raise your children. Your values must reflect the presence of God in your life. You may be a corporate executive in a competitive world. Your decisions and character must be of the highest standard. Remember Daniel in Babylon? He was second to the king, a position of great influence in that kingdom. Many around him were jealous and sought to find fault with him. Here is the outcome.

> Then the high officials and the satraps sought to find a ground for complaint against Daniel with regard to the kingdom, but they could find no ground for complaint or any fault, because he was faithful, and no error or fault was found in him. (Dan. 6:4 ESV)

Chapter 22

Work Smart

You know what you are good at. You are gifted and have skills. You know what spurs you on when you work at it. You love it and enjoy it. Do that, and you will work smart. You are not forced. You have the urge, and you do it. Many of us don't because circumstances are such that we don't do those things about which we are passionate. Some people need to dig a bit deeper to find out. For others, they are afraid that they may not succeed and that their talent may not put food on the table, lest they botch it and find no success.

We have no faith in the things that God intended for us to do from the beginning. As we race against time, we have on our agenda items that ought not to be there. Sometimes it is work we are not good at; it is not where our heart is. We find ourselves bored stiff doing the things that we don't love. Does that ring a bell? Going by the three-year assignment alluded to in this book, we then spend that time unfulfilled and unable to accomplish God's purpose in our lives. You see, Jesus knew from the very start what he was meant to do. This allowed him to go full steam ahead as soon as he started his work. He hit the ground running because he was clear on the purpose for which he had come to this earth. Are you clear? Are you dithering? It is time to go back to the drawing board before it is too late.

In 1992, a word of confirmation came to me. "Now that you are skilled in writing, write Christian literature." I had done materials development and written books for schools, but this was specific. This was a call for me to utilise the skills that I had acquired for the sake of the kingdom. This may sound strange to some. It took me over twenty years to come up with my first Christian book. This one will be my third. In that twenty years, I put aside what God wanted me to do – my purpose, my gift. What a waste of time, what a lack of faith, what procrastination. Sad. And I don't want you to do the same. Imagine how many books I would have written in those twenty years. How many lives may have been impacted? This is the greatest challenge Jesus gives us. He worked smart because he knew what he wanted to do. He lived a balanced life because he was able to prioritise.

We live in a world that is fast moving. There is the desire to make ends meet, to work tirelessly for ourselves and for our families. And yet, many times we lose focus. We have no time to reflect on what it is we can do best. We don't use time to focus on God, family, and our health. It has become a rat race – accumulation at any cost while sacrificing quality of life. When you work smart, you are at the controls. You decide and are deliberate about what you are doing. You prioritise, and you set your own agenda. You do the things that God has purposed in your heart to do, and you do them well.

Paul did the same. He had a purpose and a mission to accomplish. He had a goal to reach. He had a God to know, and he had protégés to mentor. When his time was up, he was able to say that he had accomplished the task given to him.

The irony is that books have been written, seminars have been held, and there are many motivational speakers urging people to invest now for tomorrow. They talk about how to become a millionaire, and how to think like a millionaire. There are books on the secrets of successful people and what they do. This is all impressive, but one thing is lacking. Very few have argued the importance of investing in the invisible – in a life full of contentment, joy, peace, and love. This has eluded many people, and they often shy away from talking about it. They are embarrassed. Governments have invested in today and missed the value of investing in the science of behaviour, in change and transformation of attitudes.

The parables of the kingdom told by Jesus are an eye-opener and point us to what we must do if we are going to enjoy the benefits of today and tomorrow. Many people are astute investors when it comes to investing for today, and they are not so smart when it comes to investing in tomorrow. This is why Jesus talks about the wise and the foolish – people who will only look at the present and completely overlook tomorrow. This has been the pattern of the world.

The volatility of the marketplace has not made people aware that in the space of a day, the market can crash, and all their investments can be wiped out. Many people have taken their lives because of losing on the stock exchange. Jesus warned against investing only in the material things that we see, at the expense of the unseen. He gives the example of a rich man who had everything and finally decided to invest in his warehouse so that he could sit back and relax. How foolish. Here is the full story.

> Then he said, "This is what I will do: I will tear down my barns and build larger ones, and there I will store all my grain and my goods. And I will say to my soul, 'Soul, you have many goods laid up for many years to come; take your ease, eat, drink and be merry.'" But God said to him, "You fool! This very night your soul is required of you; and now who will own what you have prepared?" (Luke 12:19 NIV)

This man did not see life beyond today, and that is why Jesus called him a fool. Jesus asks a pertinent question that many investors should ask themselves every time they want to make an investment. This is the wisdom that has eluded many. Because we look to today and are confident that today will last forever, what a surprise we have when today is erased in a huff before we realise our goal of comfort and fulfilment.

This is what astute investors should do, according to Jesus: they should be aware that anything can happen. Should it happen, they are prepared for the consequences. Where will you spend eternity if you have not invested in it? It is sad that this is overlooked by governments who have pumped millions trying to shore up ailing economies and yet have failed to invest in the ethics of living or a revamp of people's moral behaviours. They haven't put in place mechanisms that will enlarge life and ensure that we get value for money from life today and tomorrow.

Jesus presents simple criteria as a way of gaining entry into the kingdom of God. It is an acknowledgement of who he is and what he came to do. It will qualify you into the kingdom and its principles. Romans 10:9 sums it up: "If you declare with your mouth, 'Jesus is Lord,' and believe in your heart that God raised him from the dead, you will be saved" (NIV). This is straightforward and simple. You have to verbalise your entry into the kingdom. The world should know that people have decided to openly invest in tomorrow. This means that you will subscribe to the kingdom principles. Just as there are investment principles, kingdom principles govern the way kingdom business is run, and any wise investor has to familiarise himself with them. In the scheme of things, this guarantees success. A quick glance at the principles reveals how practical and down to earth these are.

These principles include entry into the kingdom, values of the kingdom, the expectations of members or citizens of the kingdom, and the destiny of those in the kingdom. How do people in the kingdom resolve issues? These values are so vital that they are worth investing in.

Jesus gives the example of a man who, when he finds treasure in a field, decides to buy the field itself. This is astute investment. You surrender all for the kingdom. Jesus gives the example of true investment when he says it is common knowledge that where your wealth is, your heart will be focused on that. You are attracted to where you have put your money. Sadly, people forget that investing in the kingdom reaps benefits and results. It guarantees peace and security. Jesus argued for investment in the kingdom when he said,

> Don't hoard treasure down here where it gets eaten by moths and corroded by rust or – worse! – stolen by burglars. Stockpile treasure in heaven, where it's safe from moth and rust and burglars. It's obvious, isn't it? The place where your treasure is, is the place you will most want to be, and end up being. (Matt. 6:19–21 MSG)

This is a clear comparison of the two types of investments there are. Jesus suggests that we do a double take on these investments and clearly show which one brings value for money. He was aware of the way investments can be wiped out when the stock market crashes and people lose billions of dollars overnight. There are always cycles of economic depression that come and go and; such volatility is the name of the game in the marketplace. Jesus comes up with an investment package that will last and survive beyond the depressions of tomorrow. This is good news. To demonstrate this, he responds to one of his disciple's concerns when the disciple put Jesus on the spot and wanted him to tell them what would happen to them now that they had left families and houses to follow Jesus. Did Jesus think this was a wise move? Here was Jesus's response.

> And everyone who has left houses or brothers or sisters or father or mother or children or lands for my name's sake. will receive a hundredfold and will inherit eternal life. (Matt. 19:29 ESV)

In effect, he was saying investment is guaranteed, now and in the future. You can't beat that! As far as Jesus was concerned, investment in the kingdom was guaranteed, and whoever took that smart decision would reap the results here on earth and also ultimately in heaven. This is no pie in the sky; it is a pragmatic decision that assures results. In 2016, Cliff Richard, following a harrowing experience in his life, said on television that his faith was stronger than ever and was never tested by the ordeal. It was not his monetary investments that got him through, but his investment in God. What a testimony.

Sometimes you wonder why many people have decided not to go that route. According to Jesus, it is a costly decision. It requires sacrifice and is not for the squeamish. It requires planning for it; you don't simply go into it without counting the cost. It can be antisocial because relationships take back stage as you seek to do what God wants you to do. It involves sleepless nights in consultation with the creator of the universe, the source of the investment. You must be prepared to wait for a return on your investment. Sometimes you will lose friends and family, especially when they don't subscribe to the commitment you made to invest in the kingdom. Many have been ostracised from their families and were made to go it alone, holding on to a faith that things will work out regardless.

Investing in the kingdom is like going against the grain. The principles that one is asked to adhere to look crazy from the outside, like loving your enemies and doing good to those who hate you. Yes, that is what investment in the kingdom means. You operate on a different level, and you tolerate things that many see as repugnant. You emulate Jesus, the author and finisher of your faith. He showed us the way to a lifetime of fulfilment. He loved when he was hated. He helped when he was not cared for. He forgave when his enemies decided to deride him and eventually kill him. He was no ordinary bloke. He was unique, and he wants those of us who seek to invest in his kingdom to do the same.

Remember Paul, the great philosopher and servant of the Lord Jesus? Once he made a commitment to follow Jesus and invest in the kingdom on the Damascus Road, he became a revolutionary for the cause of Christ. In fact, Jesus outlined to him what was ahead of him after he made that commitment. He was told in no uncertain terms that he would suffer for the cause of Christ. Suffering became one of the indicators of someone who was determined to do the will of God. It was not easy. And as we know, eventually Paul was beaten, flogged, imprisoned, and put under house arrest. Yet all this time, he continued to talk about the benefits of investing in the kingdom. His influence went far and wide through his speeches, and most important, through the many letters he wrote, which make up two-thirds of the New Testament. What an investment, and what returns! Not only is Paul in heaven, but his legacy lives on.

This is what God yearns for you. Don't be like Methusellah, who lived over nine hundred years and then died – nothing more, nothing less. We need to invest more now that we are racing against time. We need to do an audit of our lives to see where we have been and where we are going, what we have accomplished and what we hope to do for the cause of Christ. Go on, then. You are worth much more than the lilies of the field and the birds of the air. You can make a difference, and you can reap the results of your investment in this world and in the world to come.

The big question is, what are you investing in, and what returns are you expecting from your investment? You don't have to second guess what you will receive in return. The word of God is very clear about it, and it is our guide in determining what we should and should not invest in. It is the manual that all smart investors should consult if they are to realise returns on their investment. It is dynamic and sharper than a two-edged sword. We better utilise the wisdom that comes from it so that we may live. Many have neglected what God has to say through his word to their detriment – issues on marriage, success, and morality. All these are tackled in a way that brings life and stability to anyone who accepts its teaching. For example, if you want to ensure a lifelong marriage, you are urged to love your wife and submit to your husband. It outlines the various roles that God expects you to play in a relationship. Many who have heeded this call from the Bible have been successful in their marriages and have never regretted investing in the principles as given by the word of God. Many have despised them – to their peril because they have become part of the divorce statistics.

Invest more in the kingdom and expect to reap more. This is a decision that has to be taken as we go down the road to our final destination.

When you love those who don't love you, you get value for money. When you forgive those who are not forgiving, you get value for money. It changes you. You appreciate others more than yourself. You develop relationships. You neutralise your enemies and those who detest you. Even if they don't love you back, you have sown the seeds, and you reap what you have sown. Sow forgiveness, and you reap forgiveness. Sow love, and you reap love. Sow friendship, and you reap friendship. That is the kingdom. What a wonderful world it would be if that becomes the way we conduct the business of our lives.

The parable of the Good Samaritan is a clear example of how love can help reconcile those who were once distant enemies. The unheard-of becomes the norm, and people are impacted positively. The Good Samaritan defied all odds and decided to invest in doing good even though this was not done in his community. He valued the person who was beaten and battered more than the dictates of tradition. He took a risk and did what was right. The people who must have known what was right evaded the injured man and went about their business. They kept their reputations intact, but they failed to make a difference. They remained stuck in tradition and never moved on to greater things and insights.

Sadly, many of us are stuck. We have become afraid of how people will react if we take the plunge into the unknown and unacceptable. We see today and not tomorrow. We lose the importance of valuing others. We become selfish – unlike Jesus, who was selfless. We become proud and conceited – unlike Jesus, who was humble. In order to accomplish his mission, Jesus identified with the people he was going to rescue. He became a nobody in order to become a somebody, and it worked. God recognised such sacrifice, and his name was above all the other names. Why wouldn't anyone want to invest more in the kingdom when such positive returns on the investment are predicted? But many don't because they are stuck in their mindset. What is required is a paradigm shift to take on the opportunities and make a difference.

Chapter 23

The Three-Year Assignment Strategy

You have three years, and you can do likewise. The Son of God did. Let's examine his strategy for a moment. He had a mission from the start, a goal he always focused on. He declared at the beginning his priorities.

For the Son of Man came to seek and to save the lost. (Luke 19:10)

For even the Son of Man came not to be served but to serve, and to give his life as a ransom for many. (Mark 10:45)

Entry to that kingdom required people to meet certain standards. He then declared that he had come to seek and save the lost. He did not come to be served, but to serve and give his life as a ransom for many. His was a rescue plan for mankind. He decided from the outset that he would not do it singlehandedly but would require the assistance of other people. Jesus was clear on his goals, his strategy. He was not going to achieve this by his own power, but through the power of God his father. In fact, all he did was mandated by the father. There was an authority behind it – hence the confidence to do all he did in the face of many obstacles.

Here is a clear example of how to complete an assignment in the short space of three years. You need a goal, a mandate that's clear and simple. On whose authority you are doing what you are doing? Have a strategy, the how of achieving the goal. What are the resources you need? Craft the action plan and the operationalisation of the strategy. Armed with this, we see Jesus clearly fulfilling his mission, and in no time he had accomplished that mission.

Prior to the implementation of the strategy, Jesus had thirty years to prepare. We are not told in detail what happened from the time he was born to the time that he actively went around talking about the Good news. A man called John the Baptist, who spoke about Jesus's coming, did the same thing. Until he came out of the desert to tell the world that Jesus was the Messiah, he was dormant somewhere in the desert. "And the child grew and became strong in spirit; and he lived in the wilderness until he appeared publicly to Israel (Luke 1:80 NIV).

When John the Baptist came on the scene to do his mission, he made an impact, and I am sure people were amazed at his boldness and his no holds barred approach. Yet God had prepared him in the desert. It was possible for John to accomplish his ministry for the short duration because of what had gone on before. You see, it is possible to do our assignment for the specified time, but it's equally important that we prepare ourselves before we launch the ministry. What are you doing to prepare yourself, to develop yourself, to arm yourself with the necessary tools to confront any obstacles during your three-year assignment like Jesus did?

Paul, the great missionary in the New Testament, did the same thing. He had an encounter with Jesus on the road to Damascus and was plunged into God's work, in a field where some missionaries like Peter had seen Jesus face to face. But in Galatians 1, Paul reveals his preparation secret. He went into Arabia for two years. There in the desert, he must have had an encounter with God. What happened in Arabia is a matter for conjecture, but it is certain that that was his training ground. He must have had time to pray, reflect, and converse with God before he embarked on his ministry. That became the launching pad for his ministry.

It doesn't just happen – it is hard work. It is all about preparation, preparation, preparation. This is the challenge today. How prepared are you for the work that lies ahead? How much are you willing to invest today for the success of tomorrow?

Be careful of time wasters. How many times have you been bogged down in controversies and arguments that do not edify? Even after you have won the argument, you still feel awful; you have accomplished nothing. Delve into those things that help you reach your destiny. Associate with people who bring value to you. They may be rich or poor, but what they say will contribute towards your own personal development. Gossip is a time waster – even sophisticated gossip! It starts with, "Don't get me wrong, I have nothing against them, but this is what they do. I really don't like it!" Then you start talking about the negative side of people. So much time is spent concentrating on them that you have little productive things to do. Before you know it, an hour flies past. Alternatively, you could start praying for them, or seek ways to help them deal with their weaknesses. The thing is, there is not much time to waste. We need to constantly check our conversation temperature gauges to help us keep on track. Keep asking, "Is it edifying or not? Is it building someone's character or destroying it?"

Jesus was smart. Whenever he was confronted by the opposition, he never followed up with negative comments. He went on with his work in order to fulfil his mission. He knew if he did comment, he would be distracted and would never complete his task on time. Anything that you deem insignificant should be left out as you concentrate on things that have serious consequences to your plan.

Keep on Message

The 2016 US presidential elections will always be remembered for both the right and wrong reasons. But one thing both campaigns kept drumming in their candidates was that they should keep on message. The temptation was for candidates to go off at a tangent and not focus on the key messages that they wanted the electorate to hear. Jesus was a master at keeping on message. He was hardly distracted and kept focused; this enabled him to do what he did in three short years. This is our challenge as well.

We are racing against time – God's time. This is why we must be wise in whatever we do, always cognisant of the fact that it is God's time. You cannot replenish it; once it is given, it is gone. Put another way, we are all allocated a certain number of years on this beautiful planet. In fact, the Bible says on average, it is three score and an extra ten years if we are fortunate. We know that in some countries, people can now live up to one hundred years. However long our time is, it's not limitless. That is why it is important to do those things that one sets out to do within the limited time one has. You can either be wise or foolish. Refuse to do anything and just glide away aimlessly until the clock stops, or live on purpose. Be resolute and focused, and seek to achieve much not for yourself but for posterity. In modern jargon, this is called legacy – the art of passing on the baton to the next generation once your clock has run out of steam.

Let's examine Jesus's strategy from the very beginning. He followed protocol and did not want to upset the system. John was baffled when he saw Jesus coming to be baptised. He said, "Excuse me, are you out of your mind? You are supposed to baptise me, not you." Not so with Jesus. He started his work immediately. He did not dally and did not wait until he had a following. He did not consult but relied on his mandate from God. For example, there were no interviews done for Team Jesus. He simply saw them doing business in their professions and asked them to follow him. The job was offered there and then. And of course, the Bible says that Jesus had spent the whole night praying before he made the decision on whom to appoint to this important task. Again, it is preparation, preparation, preparation. He did not shy away from the opposition, be it physical or spiritual. Jesus encountered a demon-possessed man in the synagogue.

> They went to Capernaum, and when the Sabbath came, Jesus went into the synagogue and began to teach. The people were amazed at his teaching, because he taught them as one who had authority, not as the teachers of the law. Just then a man in their synagogue who was possessed by an impure spirit cried out, "What do you want with us, Jesus of Nazareth? Have you come to destroy us? I know who you are – the Holy One of God!" (Mark 1:21–24)

When confronted with someone with mental health issues, Jesus met that person's need. He was a people person, and communication was one of his greatest strategies to enable him to get his message across. He was there with the people, and of course, compassion was what drove him. He could not rescue a people without loving and caring for them.

He was practical. He cared. He coached, delegated, and showed acts of mercy. The list goes on. He used his time wisely. Amazing what Jesus was able to do in three years. All of us can make a difference in that time. Work on it.

CHAPTER 24

Choose Life

Life is all about decisions, both short term and long term. It is the small and simple decisions that we make every day that make a difference between life and death, success or failure, happiness or sadness, achieving and not achieving. At face value, choosing life sounds like something that everyone will hop on to. Let's face it: who does not want to live, breathe, and enjoy what Mother Earth has to offer? Yet many of us have put on blinders, and that simple truth has evaded us for a long time. For some, it will be a surprise when they fail to reach the goal and falter along the way.

What you decide today will affect how you live tomorrow. This is why it is important to consider every decision carefully and to go through it with a fine-tooth comb. It matters because the devil is in the details. For many of us, we live in regret for the foolish decisions we made only because we were not exposed to the philosophy that decisions direct our course of action. Many of our decisions have been taken lightly and sometimes impulsively. These decisions are in different categories: personal, corporate, peer pressure, and sometimes national decisions that call for a consensus in tackling a particular problem.

Lack of exposure to the art of decision making has contributed towards people's lack of reflection and action when it comes to decision making. A decision to marry someone, for example, is one of the most important decisions after the decision to choose where one will spend eternity. No parent has a curriculum that teaches children to know what to take into account before making such a decision – whom to consult, when to make the move, and what to do when the gear needs disengaging because of incompatibility. Many lives have been irreparably destroyed because someone took the wrong decision. Sometimes even when this is repaired, it leaves lifelong, indelible marks on one's life.

What is the most important decision you have to make today? What are the likely implications of that decision? What must you take into account as someone who is racing against time? Once I made the decision that my wife was the one I should marry, it took her two years to consider, reflect, and finally be in sync with my decision. I nearly gave up on her, but it was worth the wait!

CHAPTER 25

Focus on Your Destination

The old adage "If you don't know where you are going, any road goes" is true. Getting to one's destination requires focus. You must know where you are going, how you will get there, and the means to get there. You have a dogged determination to beat all odds until you get where you are going. All programmes and everything it takes is focused on the destination. It is important to find out what is required and when it is required. You see the end from the beginning. You proactively do things in order to realise your dream. You don't wait. You anticipate any risks and obstacles.

One of the disciples of Jesus revealed his ignorance after three years with the master when he said, "We don't know where you are going." What ? This must have taken Jesus by surprise. After so many years of coaching, teaching, and guidance, how could the man fail to know where they were heading? When he enrolled with Jesus, where did he think the road was taking him? Unfortunately, this is the response from many people. They don't know where they are going. Some even think there is no destination; they are simply walking down the road with no end in mind. How pathetic.

Fortunately for Thomas, Jesus gave him a straight answer when he said, "I am the way, the truth and the life, no one comes to the Father except through me." The journey begins and ends with God himself. The journey ends in paradise or heaven; it ends in the presence of God. Jesus was the first to get there before us so that he could prepare a place for us. Wow!

We all need to settle some questions first. Where are we going? Are we able to visualise the destination? Doing this inspires us and gets our adrenaline going as we live life with expectations of what is going to be and look forward to getting there. We run the race with determination, knowing what prize is awaiting us when we get there. It motivates us to overcome the obstacles along our way. Jesus talks about the wide road and the narrow road. Those who are destined for the destination are usually on the narrow road. It represents the struggles and stamina required for those who have made a decision to choose life.

This road is characterised by pain, trials, and temptations. It requires tenacity, patience, and courage. This is why few people are on this road at one time. Every day, prospective candidates for the destination should brace themselves for a life of discipline as they look forward to being in the kingdom of God. Jesus made a very fundamental statement when he said, "Many are called but few are chosen." This implies that for many who do not endure until the end, they may miss the boat and are not able to get there. Although the invitation is open to everyone, it is important to abide by what Jesus says if entrance to that kingdom is going to be guaranteed. It is not a free-for-all. It is not for the fearful, but for the strong and courageous. It is for those who obey what the master says and who seek always to please him. It is for those who have put Jesus at the pinnacle of their lives. To them, he is the commander in chief!

You can only focus on the destination if you know where it is, what is required, and how to prepare yourself to meeting the standards of entry to that destination. The history of salvation from the beginning has revealed how God intended from the beginning to have fellowship with man and to seek to bring him into his presence. But his first attempts did not succeed, because man rebelled against God. Finally, Jesus came on to the scene. He became as we are in order to rescue those who were outside and who were not guaranteed God's destination. God has made it possible for everyone to get to the destination and be assured of entry into it – as long as they acknowledge him as Lord and saviour, as long as they obey and do what he tells them to do. This is no big deal because God has provided all the resources to enable every man and woman to do this. Confidence about the destination is assured as long as you adhere to what Jesus says.

Victory is assured because God has promised to take care of us. At one point before he left the earth, Jesus said, "In the world you will face persecution, but take heart, I have overcome the world" (John 16:13 NIV). This is reassuring. It means that although we cannot escape the troubles and tribulations of this world, we have an assurance that God is on our side, and we shall overcome.

Today, the world is a challenging environment: wars, bombings, uprisings, and moral decadence. We are called upon to live in such a world and still find our way to our ultimate destination. For some, it is not going to be easy. Many have lost loved ones through terrorism, tsunamis, and the like. Many have found no solace in their workplaces, and they cannot make ends meet. But the promise still stands. The hope still lingers. As long as you remain focused, getting there will not be an issue.

What do people who focus on their destination do? They keep on keeping on. They remain determined. They do the best they can to rally others around them and excite them about where they are going. They are not embarrassed to tell others about it. They are resilient and are patient because they realise it takes walking without fainting to get there. It requires vigilance, lest you are sidetracked and lose focus. They are confident because they know in whom they believe. They count everything as rubbish for the sake of reaching their destination. In the Bible, Paul was so determined to reach his destination that he made these remarks.

> What is more, I consider everything a loss because of the surpassing worth of knowing Christ Jesus my Lord, for whose sake I have lost all things. I consider them garbage, that I may gain Christ. (Phil. 3:8 NIV)

Now *that* is determination. That is focus. All else pales in significance because of the big prize along the way. You cannot afford to cloud your vision if you want to get to your destination. You must do that one thing that will catapult you to the destination. You must set your priorities right. Many heroes of the faith did this, and they were victorious.

This radical approach was adopted by Jesus. He gives the example of someone ploughing the land who decides to look back. Jesus deems that person unsuitable for the kingdom of God. The reason? Looking back takes you away from the goal, the destination. He even says that there will have to be sacrifices. You may lose some quality time with people because of your passion and zeal for the end game. In fact, Jesus talks of a new type of family: those who do the will of he who sent him are his real brothers and sisters. They are bound by the same mission, the same goal, and a similar focus. Together, you can share the frustrations and difficulties on the road to where you are going. It is no good flocking together with people who do not share your vision, be they family or friends.

Getting to one's destination, just like achieving a goal, demands a strategy. It needs a deliberate set of alternatives to help achieve the objectives with minimum disruption. It means being proactive instead of being reactive, It is about preventing the fire instead of firefighting, and being aggressive instead of being retrogressive. Go for it instead of retreating into your cul-de-sac. Be preemptive, have a go-getter attitude, and be alert and vigilant.

Life is deliberate; it doesn't just happen. You have to be in charge and not be a passenger. You must set priorities and not merely procrastinate. Life must be results oriented and productive, and you can't wait to consume and enjoy others' sweat and blood.

Sadly, many people simply exist from the cradle to the grave, and the grave becomes the end, with nothing beyond that. Some people wait for things to happen instead of making things happen. That is not enough. Jesus is a classic example of someone who was a go-getter and who never wavered from his mission. "I work while it is day for the night is coming. My work is to do the will of him who sent me." Jesus came, and he was certain he would go back to the one who had sent him. We were born for a purpose, and after that is fulfilled, we are on our way to the one who sent us.

What is your destination? How do you get there, and what do you need to do in order to get there? What are some of the obstacles that you are likely to face in order to achieve your objective? These are the questions at the forefront of those of us who live in expectation of the time when we will get out of this planet and go beyond the galaxies to a "land where joy shall never end". Call it heaven, call it paradise, but in essence this is where God is – his presence.

CHAPTER 26

Where will You Spend Eternity?
(Your Long-term Investment)

I am the way the truth and the life, no one comes to the Father except through me.

—John 14:6 NIV

This is the crux of the matter for many people, because your decision will decide your destiny. The answer to this question should trigger a series of responses that will not only impact your present but also set you up to arrive at your future with expectation. It is a pauser; it begs reflection and is worth considering. In all his ministry, Jesus was preoccupied with making sure that people knew where they were going based on the decisions they made in this life. It is no different today. You may deliberately decide to put this question in the back burner, but it will keep popping up and won't go away. Stories have been told of people who never considered a response to this question, desperately seeking to do so on their death beds.

When you are racing against time, ultimately your response to where you are going and why is of critical importance.

Eternity is the timeless period after death where those who have made a decision to become members of the kingdom of God will be. It is paradise re-enacted, a place of bliss and God's presence will be, and it's infinite. Revelation 7 talks about it as a land where there is no hunger or thirst. God is sitting on the throne and is surrounded by people worshipping him day and night. The flip side is another existence of doom and gloom, popularly known as hell, for those who have decided not to become members of the kingdom. It is described as "eternal damnation" where there is "the gnashing of teeth or perpetual suffering". One way or the other, it exists to welcome those who will have made a decision either way. This is the stark choice that is presented to all mankind, and it is for the taking – not by imposition, but by choice.

Our daily choices are always tainted by our constant reflection on the global picture of the purpose for our being. The destination looms large as we consider each day the wise things we have to undertake. In most cases, these are affected by what we have chosen to pursue. At the back of our minds, there is a deliberate reminder of what it is we must do in order to enable us to realise the ultimate goals we have set ourselves. Whether or not people believe in the afterlife, deep down there is a constant spiritual battle, and this should affect anyone's regular discourse on what they should do and how they should behave.

What you envisage the future to hold for you, and what you expect to reap out of it, affects how you conduct yourselves daily. It determines the way you act, the habits you form, and the disciplines you are willing to endure as you seek to attain your goal. Just like any successful people who set different courses of action to achieve their goals, you are faced with this fundamental question.

What strategies do you require to put into place in order for you to live, behave, and work in accordance with what your destiny demands? There is no running away from the fact that you will allow influences that will only help you achieve what you set out to achieve. You cannot expect to spend your life in eternity when you have not adequately prepared for it. The children of Israel were delivered from Egypt, and God promised them Canaan, "a land flowing with milk and honey". This was a journey with a purpose. They had to meet God's standards along the way; otherwise, they would not reach their destination. Their behaviour, responses, and general conduct under the leadership of Moses contributed to the success or failure of their journey.

They had to remain focused. They had to adhere to God's rigid discipline. They were to meet the standards God set. Obedience was always their mantra. Sadly, many of those who left Egypt and who were over twenty years of age failed to make it to Egypt. The reason? They did not meet the standard set by God, and they were disobedient. Instead of appreciating what God was doing and what he had done, they complained and disappointed God. Even their leader, Moses, failed to make the final grade. God said to him, "Because you did not behave holy in front of my people, you shall not enter Canaan." However, God gave Moses a preview of the land of promise by getting him on Mount Nebo so that he could look across and see Canaan.

The people of Israel had to keep their eyes on the ball all the time. They could not afford to slacken and be distracted from their mission. God had warned them that on their journey, there would be many obstacles, including nations that would fight them. Nations also did not believe in their God, who would present to them different forms of worship. They refrained from giving in to such abominable practices if they were to achieve their goal.

Where you will spend eternity depends on how far you have embraced what you have been given as the standard. Jesus did not mince words. If you treat him as Lord and saviour, and if you believe in what he came to do, then your future is guaranteed. You became unique, and your interests are renewed. Your talk is seasoned with salt, your mind is transformed, and you no longer conform to the world. As the Message Bible says,

> Don't become so well-adjusted to your culture that you fit into it without even thinking. Instead, fix your

attention on God. You'll be changed from the inside out. (Rom. 12:2 MSG)

You now fix your attention on God. He is the one who will ensure that your life along the journey will be changed from the inside out. You'll be a new person for a new goal and on a new journey. This becomes your preparation for the prize ahead. The reward is reserved for those who are purposeful about their lives, who are not rolling stones that gather no moss. It's a destination with clear guidelines on how to get there, what to do on the way there, and the consequences to be faced if one wanders away from the stipulated direction.

Where will you spend eternity? That motivates and inspires you, and you can better focus on your goal. It motivates because every day, you want to make sure that whatever you do adds up towards the goal. Nothing is done aimlessly – it is deliberate and strategic. Your daily routine reflects a person on a mission. Your to-do list on a daily basis involves meaningful steps towards the intended goals. It may be writing a book, like I am doing now, with the intention of influencing others for the good. It may be going to the gym as an investment in your health, which ensures that you live a productive life and that your creative juices can flow unabated. It could be involvement in the Church as part of the body of Christ; this ensures that you help influence many to embrace the cause of Christ, thereby building their character. As you add up these purposeful acts each day, you drive away anxiety, depression, and any feelings of despondency because you are always on the move. You act with a purpose. You drive away gossip and irrelevant associations that may easily distract you from your intended course.

Where you will spend eternity inspires you, because you can see the end from the beginning. You can prepare what is to come before it finally arrives. You are able to plan each day in accordance with the standard guidelines that God has given you in the Bible. It is not a guessing game; the answers to the question are provided already. All you need to do is study the answers and do exactly what you are told. The key is to be consistent and patient, to stay focused towards the goal, and to live in expectation. This will keep you going and will spur you on even when the going is tough. Many of those who have given up have not looked forward towards the mark. Paul realised this when he said,

> Not that I have already obtained or have already become perfect, but I press on so that I may lay hold of that for which also I was laid hold of by Christ Jesus. Brethren, I do not regard myself as having laid hold of it yet; but one thing I do: forgetting what lies behind and reaching forward to what lies ahead. (Phil. 3:12 NIV)

This eternity mindset keeps you going, and you press on until the end. It is a prize worth winning, worth dying for. Many heroes of the Bible had a similar mindset. Hebrews says this about them.

They were stoned, they were sawn in two, they were tempted, they were put to death with the sword; they went about in sheepskins, in goatskins, being destitute, afflicted, ill-treated men of whom the world was not worthy, wondering in deserts and mountains and caves and holes in the ground. These were all commended for their faith, yet none of them received what had been promised. (Heb. 11:37–39 NIV)

This is what an eternity mindset does when it is grounded in faith. You are fearless because you have such faith in the one who has promised eternity. You cannot let go because you are sure you will attain it. Sometimes, like these heroes of the faith, it was not achieved in their lifetimes but after they left the planet. This is why many who are grounded in this faith are confident that they will make it. Living or dying is neither here or there; it doesn't matter anymore. They are prepared, just like Paul could face challenges head-on and expect results because of his faith in God, who is mighty. What a difference this would make to our world if we all had such faith, tenacity, and endurance. We'd have the ability to declare our commitment to God, such that we were not fearful any more. We'd have the realisation that whatever happens, we would spend the rest of our lives in eternity. Our future was secure.

This song explains the question of eternity and the importance of knowing your stance on it. It is upon reflection that we realise how seriously we must take each step in our journey towards eternity.

Where will you spend eternity?
This question comes to you and me!
Where will you spend eternity?
Eternity, Eternity.
Where will you spend eternity?

Words by Elisha A. Hoffman

Music by John H. Tenney

The End

As we race against time, it is important that we reflect on this fundamental question. The ball is in our court. We can be guaranteed acceptance in the kingdom because of what Jesus has done. This is no mystery, but it's a clear response to the one who created heaven and earth. It is a matter of choice, and there is no imposition. The time is now. The thief on the cross with Jesus made his decision in the nick of time, and he was guaranteed paradise there and then – guaranteed. There were no ifs or buts, and he got a straight answer. His desire was granted, and he knew where he would spend eternity. Wow!

What are you working towards? What is your life's goal, and what is your destination? It is important to capture these thoughts every day because they will affect what we do on a daily basis – whether you have a purpose driven life or a purposeless life, whether you utilise your gifts and talents towards your long-term goal, or your gifts are lying dormant within you.

By writing this book, I have decided to put my skills and talents to good use. Your reading this book is evidence of its importance to you, and hopefully it will have an impact on your life. Each time I have sat to write, I have remained focused and have been able to ward off thoughts and influences that destroy and do not build. I have made good use of my time and contributed towards my eternity goal by influencing others towards the same. The parable of the talents told by Jesus is very relevant here. Of the three who were given talents, one decided not to do something about it. He wasted time and brought no return on the investment. It's no wonder why he got punished for it, because wasted time is unproductive time. We cannot afford to do that when we are racing against time.

Be clear about your purpose. Be clear about your destination, and your life will become worthwhile. What a difference you will make to those around you. The race is on – today!

Printed in the United States
By Bookmasters